Contents

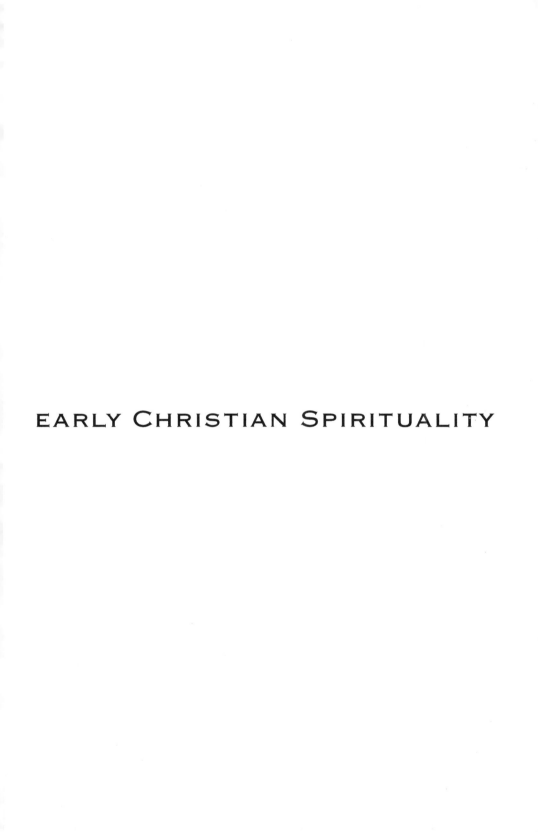

EARLY CHRISTIAN SPIRITUALITY

David Torkington has sold over 450,000 books
and been translated into 12 languages.
BOOKS BY DAVID TORKINGTON

*Never Too Late to Love – Our La-
dy's Sublime Teaching on Prayer*

Inner Life – A Fellow Traveller's Guide to Prayer

A New Beginning – A Sideways Look at the Spiritual Life

The Primacy of Loving – The Spirituality of the Heart

Wisdom from the Western Isles – The Making of a Mystic

*Wisdom from the Christian Mystics –
How to Pray the Christian Way*

Wisdom from Franciscan Italy – The Primacy of Love

How to Pray – A Practical Guide to the Spiritual Life

Prayer Made Simple – CTS booklet

Dear Susanna – It's Time for a Christian Renaissance

EARLY CHRISTIAN SPIRITUALITY

2nd Edition

Formerly Entitled: Family Spirituality

DAVID TORKINGTON

ESSENTIALIST
PRESS

Essentialist Press
Coeur d'Alene, ID 83815
www.EssentialistPress.com

Paperback ISBN 978-1-965801-03-1

Hardcover ISBN 978-1-965801-04-8

eBook ISBN 978-1-965801-05-5

To the Moreau family,
Ryan and Kelsey, and their five children,
Lily, Lila, Presley, Poppy and Patrick

Foreword – Kevin Wells

On this cold winter morning in America, my Irish imagination has prodded into my mind an image of David Torkington. I see the old Englishman slowly fading away, disappearing on a windswept field. Small pieces of him are breaking apart and lifting into the breezy sky, similar to a winter-forgotten scarecrow vanishing in the winds of a snow-covered cornfield. My eyes well up now. I imagine I feel this way for the same reason sadness overcomes a five-year-old boy looking out of a car window watching a solitary scarecrow disintegrating in a frozen field. From the back seat, with eyes unstained by the sin of the world, the boy sees the lonely and broken-hearted scarecrow from the heart of his own soul.

Torkington is this scarecrow.

For more than half of a century he has stood like a bruised reed, alone, in the dead center of the wild plain of a Catholic Church that has mostly dismissed mystical prayer. Although the world starves - perhaps today more than ever before - for union with an unseen God, Church leaders and clergy have mostly discarded the greatest tool to attain that mystic union. Decade after decade, Torkington has leaned into stiff winds of resistance in order to ward off crows, the circling vultures, and unseen demons to herald the centuries-old solution to the acceleration of what often seems a worldwide loss of

1

reason. "It is meditative prayer," he proclaims. "If I had just a day left, it is all that I'd preach. Everything now must go to—and be received—from God."

Although Torkington has written several books and numberless articles on mystical prayer and has spoken and led retreats on the Church's ancient form of prayer throughout the world, he is barely seen or listened to anymore. These "unlisteners" are like the Moms and Dads in the front seats of cars throughout the world, passing through farmland and thinking of the next thing or task - while the untainted child in the back seat sees the landscape through the eyes of his open naturally contemplative heart. Put another way, when the Church shifted to studying ways of loving God rather than just loving and contemplating Him - which it had practised with consistency since Pentecost - consideration of God as a paternal Lover of souls began to slip away. Today, perhaps, the Church has never experienced greater travail.

Thankfully, because the old rugby player is a jolly old soul with storehouses of burning embers still remaining in his belly, he is writing and speaking like never before. He would tell you as much. In our midst, at least on this early winter morning in 2024, Torkington is an 86-year-old man who knows his time on earth is coming to an end. With a Catholic Church buried in a long wintertime, he knows it is no time for him to dawdle. So, each day from his home in the wilds on the southern tip of England, he stretches out his sore back, tinkers around in his garden, and takes strolls toward the beach to keep in shape and brace himself for the whirlwind. It is tiring proclaiming the most important message in the world directly into the crosswinds of society's ever-blowing cacophony of distractions. So Torkington inhales deeply, then bellows like John the Baptist in the wilderness: I've come to know the path to the buried treasure in the field. I know where the pearl is, and I know how you can attain it. Come: Let me show you to the way of martyrs, saints, mystics, and of your ancient ancestors, who once laid their head against Christ's heart in mystical prayer and gained heaven.

The achy-boned semi-hermit has written his magnum opus in Early Christian Spirituality. Before you open to Chapter One, though, I'll suggest you make a prayer of petition to God that Torkington's omnibus on mystical prayer begins to work its way into your essence and soul. And you might want to thank God while you're at it - because in your hands is a gift that cannot be measured. This book is an aggregate of many thousands of hours of prayerful contemplation of God. It can be argued that no layman in the world today has spent more hours in meditative prayer than David Torkington. The chapters and words herein are like small constellations of shooting stars that you will find often leaves you marvelling. Early Christian Spirituality is a compilation on prayer from the soul of a man who has never stopped praying.

As a young boy growing up in post-World War II England, Torkington felt the benevolence of God's love and care for him when he was mysteriously piloted through dark days of dyslexia. He had begun to pray ceaselessly for a small miracle of clear-headed classroom comprehension and lucidity - and shortly later, the gift was given. Thereafter, little David understood God was a Father who listened to and loved poor, pleading boys like him. The student then fell in love with the notion that union with God could be attained on earth through consistent silent prayer. He was fascinated with God listening so closely to him; in fact, he began to see that God heard every syllable out of his mouth. It was certainly "first fervor", but the match was struck, and a pilot light blinked on.

The remainder of his life was given over to prayer, and the methods of learning it, or at least in the fashion where union with God could be attained. The prodigious teaching, writing, and prayer born out of his childhood experience has helped make David Torkington the world's foremost Mystical Theologian. You will find no better teacher this side of heaven. The pages before you are the synthesis of all he knows, of all God has spoken to the caverns of his heart.

If you've come to this book with a sincere desire to attain union with God in prayer - and you read Early Christian Spirituality with consideration, care, and with a working highlighter - Torkington's words might be the catalyst to take you to heaven. His kindly manner, storytelling, and readable writing style will act as handholds to escort you into the wide and wild land of mystical prayer. As you begin flipping pages, you may even begin to subliminally hear Torkington's English-accented chuckle at memories of your own first fervor. But because he remembers so well how the sweet vapours of consolation came to an abrupt end in his own life - you might sense the gravity of his love for you as you read on and begin to weigh the cost of entering into, enduring, and even flourishing in your own dark night. And when, alas, you emerge from that pitiless but purposeful place, you might feel Torkington standing invisibly beside you, waiting with a steaming cup of English tea by the hearth fire. Why might you discover him mysteriously working his way into your soul this way? Because he loves you - and he knows that on the other side of your dark night - when the Holy Spirit has propelled your soul into the shattering reaches of union with God - he wants to speak into the depths of you: You have entered the mystic way. You are the small boy in the back seat - you've become the bright Alleluia of God's purity and love. So go now, please, and show the face of Christ to an aching world that no longer knows how to prayerfully reach Him.

This book is a Last Will and Testament, a sort of summing up of the entirety of Christian spirituality. Because Torkington adores the old customs and ancient habits of prayer, he has written this A-to-Z blueprint to help bring back our vanishing and once-vibrant Catholic communities. Torkington smiles his knowing smile when rowdy folks point to Vatican II as the reason for the piecemeal Church collapse. If that person is willing to listen, though, Torkington will begin to explain how the collapse in prayer and devotion began more than 400 years ago. He traces the freefall in mystical prayer back to the rise of the false philosophy of Quietism. The Bride of Christ, he'll tell you, began to grow brittle, wither, and stray from God's heart in the 17th century more than a century after the Council of Trent. Quietism (a false mysticism), he says, injected a poisonous wave of spiritual myopia and disordered living into Catholic communities. In this book, Torkington explains the manner in which it happened, and how the philosophy has wormed so successfully into today's Church.

This book, though, is not about dark things. It acts as torchlight for readers to see past false and twisted notions of modern ideas of Catholicism. This book points to ways of beginning to build your own small communities of sacrificial love constructed on the foundation of devoted prayer. This book points you to the harmony and way of the Church's earliest Christian families.

Our long Church wintertime is why Torkington is begging harder now. Dear reader, this old man wants you to understand the urgency to find God in the silence of your personal prayer. He believes it will be holy members of the laity that will lead the Church back to a place of grace. And he will show you how you can be one of those torch bearers. One example: Torkington reveals how a prayer as short, sweet, and simple as the Morning Offering can re-route your entire life and put you on a path to sainthood. His words will carry you into the poor home in Nazareth, where he'll teach your inner eye to see Mary seated on a wooden bench praying her own Morning Offering. Meditative prayer will seat you right beside her. He will unveil and teach you the prayer lives of the Church's earliest titans and paragons.

A word of warning: This book will prove purposeless without an effort on the reader's part to begin to declutter and pull away from peripheral activities, such as mindless scrolling, social media consumption, and sloth. For God to make His home within you, Torkington encourages readers to take his writing and prayer deadly seriously. Nearly a century of his wisdom and study cannot fully take root without an inventory of one's own soul and discarding of things unnecessary and peripheral.

To begin the journey, Torkington says, meditate - slowly, slowly, slowly - on Beloved John's depiction of Christ's sacrificial love given in the Upper Room. As Jesus gave everything as the Slaughtered Lamb, you, too, should sacrifice time to hear His words in prayer. Torkington wants you to spend great amounts of time with Him in Gethsemane to see the horror in his eyes at prayer. Then see the magnitude of His Mother's pain when He collapsed bloody and beaten in front of her, with His cross on top of Him, smothering and choking Him. Through meditative prayer, Torkington says, the Holy Spirit will begin to lead you to a fuller understanding of God's intense love for you and the countless ways throughout the day that He knocks on the door of your soul.

Essentially, Early Christian Spirituality is this: Torkington has given to you seventy-five years of experience, study, and untiring prayer for a single reason: He wants to reveal the manner in which God can seep into every corner of your life.

"The Mystic Way is a pure gift from God," Torkington says. "But one can prepare the way to receive this gift through the daily practice of meditative prayer. What love desires is union, and after some time of this form of prayer, the Holy Spirit will begin to infuse you with an understanding of God's love. And that's when change happens - because the Holy Spirit has taken you into the Mystic Way."

Is Torkington your own personal Simeon in the temple - the aged and wizened one who's been waiting for you - the one aching to lead you to God? Is he the one whom we've all been waiting for in this time of societal chaos and a Church caught in pain and confusion? Is he the line-faced archetype we can gather round to keep warm during this long wintertime in the Church? Well, that's for you to decide as you read on—but after reading Early Christian Spirituality, I believe he may well be.

Why? Because he proposes and articulates what by and large the Church no longer does. He begs the laity to return to the way of prayer of the early Church—which was continually leaning one's head against the inner chamber of the heart of Christ through contemplative prayer. Until his last breath, Torkington will mourn over the Church's shunning of mystical prayer. The centuries-long shunning of Christ's own method of prayer has crushed his heart.

"Why would the Church turn away from the very prayer of Our Lady, Christ's disciples, the early martyrs, and Church Fathers? Going to the heart of God is the only solution to what ails us," he says. "It is time to return to the Spirituality that God gave us and to learn from our earliest forebears. It is so clear, so simple and so totally transforming, for it transforms us into being one with Christ."

Introduction

LEO TOLSTOY SAID that although Christian intellectuals rise to great heights in almost every branch of secular achievement, there is almost always a serious discrepancy between their academic achievement and their spiritual development. I have noticed this recently in the Catholic intellectuals who have been analysing and explaining Synodality in recent months. The steady *drip, drip, drip* of the anti-Catholic theology disseminated by the modernists in Rome might have otherwise escaped us if it were not for the vigilance and brilliant intellectual analysis of Catholic intellectuals.

However, they are unfortunately inhibited when it comes to pointing to a positive spiritual way forward. In most cases, the current decline in Catholic spirituality has meant that spiritual growth has not grown in parity with intellectual advancement. Devotional simplicity may well be both orthodox and endearing. Still, it is far from what is necessary to lead the faithful back to the profound Catholic spirituality given to us by Jesus Christ. It is not they who are to blame. Truthfully, there has not been any simple, positive, Gospel-based spirituality made available to us from the shepherds to whom the laity once sought guidance. The very few exceptions prove the rule. Even if there are some who could lead us, they dare not speak out for fear of being cancelled, as hundreds if not thousands of Catholic priests have already been cancelled by the current

8

regime in Rome and the 'Eminence Gris' with the iron hand in the velvet glove. America's beloved Bishop Strickland is just one of the latest, known to so many of us because of his simple guileless goodness, but I fear he will not be the last.

It seems that leadership is now left to the laity. But can lay leaders who have helped us to understand the takeover of our Church in Rome be expected to guide us spiritually in these times of terrible travail? Yes, I believe they can. By deepening the *sensus fidelium* that has already guided them to defend the truth, they can now guide us to the fullness of truth, which is Love. This love of God can be retrieved only by embracing the profound sacrificial spirituality and prayer of Jesus Christ. This prayer was central to the spirituality of early Christianity, and last flourished in the Church amid a spirituality that reached astounding heights in the years following the Council of Trent. Its full expression and glory were embodied in the Tridentine Mass and the attendant Tridentine spirituality that surrounded it for over a hundred years. This spirituality taught the profound sacrificial spirituality that had always taken place within the Mystical Body of Christ as believers sought to travel onward in search of divine union. St Paul called this divine union promised by God from the beginning '*The Mysterion*'.

Believers who sought to arrive at this sublime destination were called mystics, and the way upon which they travelled came to be called the 'Mystic Way' because it took place in the Mystical Body of Jesus, inspired by the mystical love of the Holy Spirit. The word *mystical* merely means *hidden, secret, unseen, or invisible*, from the Greek word *Mysterion*, which, as we have seen, St Paul used to describe God's hidden plan to share his life and love with us. However, I must warn against being misled by spiritual dilettantes, who abound everywhere today, promising bogus and bizarre forms of mysticism that are totally alien to true Catholic spirituality. The Catholic Tridentine Spirituality, to which I have referred, has for centuries been in serious decline since the 1687 condemnation of the pseudo-mysticism called Quietism. I have detailed the devilry done by the perpetrators of this heresy in my course on prayer and in my books. Its malign influence down to the present day cannot be exaggerated, most particularly because few have ever heard about it.

After its condemnation, spiritual ignoramuses, armed with the slogan 'mysticism begins in mist and ends in schism', have been throwing the baby out with the bathwater. Thus, the mystical sacrificial spirituality given to the Church by Jesus has been all but totally extracted from Catholic mainstream spirituality. As the divine unconditional, selfless loving, which pertains to the essence of Christ's own personal redemptive spirituality, has no longer been taught, there has been a void in mainstream Catholic spirituality. This void has been filled by a plethora of 'pick-and-mix' devotional exercises that provide little more than a survival diet for the spiritually needy. The Mass still remains but is sadly no longer surrounded by the profound Tridentine Spirituality that last prevailed unimpeded in the seventeenth century, as shown by Monsignor Ronald Knox in his book, *Enthusiasm*.

This spirituality perfectly mirrored and reflected the profound sacrificial spirituality that was commonplace to all in the early Church. It was and still should be a spirituality where the only form of love that can unite us with God is learnt, namely unalloyed, selfless, unconditional loving. As counterfeit Mystical Theology has been substituted for authentic Catholic Mystical Theology, counterfeit loving (lust) has been substituted for true Christlike loving. Or at least this is what our anti-traditional 'leaders in Rome' are trying to achieve.

In the past, I have always felt incapable of describing in detail, within a single article, this God-given spirituality that Christ introduced into the early Church. Thanks to Essentialist Press (www.essential-istpress.com), I have explained and developed this profound biblical spirituality in twelve free lectures on 'Prayer to Contemplation'. They are awaiting you now on the above-mentioned site. In these talks, I have detailed the historical reasons why this spirituality has been on a steady downward slope over the last four hundred years or more, leading to the moral malaise we currently find from top to bottom in the Church today. If you believe I am exaggerating, then ask yourself why tens of thousands of Cardinals, Bishops, and priests have been indulging in horrendous cases of the sexual abuse of men, women, and children for years with virtual impunity. Ask yourself why have many more members of the hierarchy been endlessly covering up these crimes? Ask yourself why do hundreds of thousands of victims remain unheard and uncared for even to the present time and to the present Pope? Ask yourself why is such sexual depravity not being stopped but rather being normalised and even sacralised? Ask yourself why has Our Lady repeatedly had to call us to repentance? Ask yourself why has she warned of imminent divine intervention and punishment because no one is seriously listening to her? Even the best of us think we can enjoy all the pleasures of this earthly world while receiving all the graces of the heavenly world to come.

After the Renaissance and the birth of the modern world, a man-centred spirituality gradually took centre stage and pushed into the wings the God-centred spirituality Christ gave us. The Credo of the God-given spirituality that Christ gave us is, 'I believe in God, and in his Salvation through the wisdom that he has given us'. The Credo of the man-centred spirituality that man has given himself is, 'I believe in Man, in his Salvation, through the wisdom of the world that we have learnt for ourselves'. Without the selfless, unconditional loving that Christ asks of us, our Catholic spirituality is in dire straits. It cannot thrive with the self-centred, woke and wanton wisdom of the world taking centre stage, promising a new secular world order called Globalism.

In the New World Order that Marx once visualised, the suppressed proletariat would be inflamed to rise and overcome the establishment. But the once suppressed proletariat are no more. True to his spirit, however, the would-be new order in the Catholic Church has turned to the long-since suppressed sexual seditionists to rise from amongst their ranks to overcome two thousand years of sacred tradition. Their presence is everywhere apparent, thanks to the weak, chipboard spirituality that has been evident almost everywhere in the Catholic Church. This spirituality has progressively developed over the years since genuine selfless mystical loving has been undermined in the wake of the condemnation of Quietism, the pseudo-self-gratifying sexual mysticism.

Let us all begin again to turn back to God and embrace the simple but profound form of sacrificial spirituality Christ has given to us. In doing so, a formidable Remnant will be formed before the next round of anti-traditional teachings are unleashed. I appeal to all those good Catholic intellectuals who have helped us understand the pernicious takeover of our beloved Church to take upon themselves a further role. Despite their brilliant work, we now know that only God can help us in this last minute of extra time. *Prayer* is merely the word we use to describe how we radically turn to him now and without delay. We need lay leadership to lead us all back to the deep, sacrificial prayer first embodied in the prayer life of Christ, through which he redeemed the world. We look to these lay leaders for inspiration and spiritual guidance. I have written this book with those lay leaders in mind. We must remember that for three hundred years, long before any religious orders were dreamt of the family that was the basic spiritual powerhouse of the Church and the springboard for apostolic action. This action, propelled by love generated in Catholic families by the Holy Spirit, transformed a pagan Roman Empire into a Christian Empire in such a short time. We need to be taught again how to draw strength from the graces of married life and turn to prayer without delay. The main problem is that the word and the practice of prayer have been so depreciated and so devalued in the last three hundred years that even some of our most valued lay leaders fail to see its importance. Therefore, I have produced this and other books, my free course on prayer, and several podcasts which detail how Christ himself prayed in order to sacralise each day by offering it to God, presenting an example to us all.

I refer to the sacrificial prayer, as practised by Christ himself during his life on earth, which has been handed on to us by both word and example. God is indeed asking lay leaders to become great journalists, commentators, and analysts, yet he is also calling them to be spiritual leaders, too. With their professional expertise yoked to an ever-growing life of prayer, they can become the leaders the Church so desperately needs today. By now, it should be realised that even the most brilliant criticism and the most bold presentation of truth to power is not enough. Only by the power of God's Love working through us can we retrieve what has been lost and put back what needs to be reinstated. *Prayer* is merely the word used to describe how we receive it.

After over sixty years of studying and trying to live and write about the perennial Catholic teaching on prayer, I gradually realised that no one was really interested. The prevailing spirit of Pelagianism, which is the besetting sin of Modernists, has for too long made all too many believers think they can do for themselves what only the Holy Spirit can achieve, working through 'the poor and humble of heart'. For those who have finally begun to realise that what is happening in Rome can only be undone not by them but by the Holy Spirit, I have produced my twelve-part course on prayer; thanks again to Essentialist Press.

Christ will reign victorious in the final battle ahead. That is certain! Whether or not we will be on his side to savour that victory is another matter. The course is open to you now for free does not contain any gimmicks, nor is it my work, but the God-given sacrificial spirituality first lived and practised by Our Lord Jesus Christ before he gave it to his Church, through those first apostles, who unlike all too many of their successors today, died rather than deny it.

David Torkington: Ash Wednesday 2024

CHAPTER 1

The Birth of a Mystical Spirituality

WHILST THE FIRST GOOD FRIDAY was a world-shaking victory for one man, it seemed a total failure to others. All their hopes, dreams, and plans had been shattered as a pall of doom and gloom enveloped the very foundation of their beings. Nevertheless, what happened on the first Pentecost day totally revived them; all their hopes, dreams, and plans were now back on the drawing board. Jesus Christ, whom they loved so deeply and dearly before his terrible crucifixion, had not only risen from the dead, as they saw for themselves but much more. He had been so glorified with his Father's love that he could now share it with them as he promised and with the three thousand others who, seeing what his love was doing for his disciples, wanted to receive it for themselves.

The Church now existed in all its simplicity. All the external, physical, and spiritual ramifications would grow from what was little more than a mustard seed at the beginning until it transformed the largest empire the world had ever known, into a Christian Empire. This growth happened so swiftly that, even today, secular historians struggle to explain how a small dissident Jewish sect could infiltrate and overtake a massive pagan empire so quickly.

Unlike any other prior religion, this new religion did not depend purely on human love but on the love of God. Like all love, God's

15

love can be instantly experienced, as they experienced it on the first Pentecost day. But it would take many months, and even years, for it to percolate and penetrate the very marrow of their beings. This spiritual growth would ultimately enable them to receive in full measure what they initially received only in a limited measure. The first Christians practised a way of life they simply called 'The Way' in which they received God's love endlessly poured out by their Risen Lord. They called this the spiritual life because the love of the Risen Lord was none other than the Holy Spirit, the One whose love had bonded the Father to the Son from eternity. It was because this Way could not be seen, nor could the spiritual striving of those who were in 'The Way', that it gradually came to be called the 'Mystic Way', meaning invisible or unseen because of the secret journey upon which the first Christians were engaged was hidden from outsiders. However, its effects could nevertheless be seen in those who practised it.

Because this Way could only advance to the degree and to the measure that spiritual travellers are united with their Risen Lord, this journey involves an ongoing purification. The imperfect cannot be united with the perfect until there is a sufficient likeness for the One to be united with the other. In subsequent centuries, when the initially vibrant faith gradually grew cold, the importance of a mystical purification was completely forgotten, at least in practice as it is today.

The reason why this happened, and how this Mystical Spirituality can return so that Christ can do through us for the modern pagan world what He did through the ancient pagan world is the subject of this book. May readers not be seduced by false modesty to believe that this task would not include someone as spiritually or morally weak or as intellectually challenged as themselves. Remember St Paul, who said God's power works best in weakness. Remember those simple, uneducated men whom Christ originally chose to do what he would like to do again through us.

An early Philosopher and a major opponent of the Church called Celsus criticised many of the first Christians because they were a bunch of deplorables culled from the dregs of society. Gradually, the highly educated, intellectual, and sophisticated Roman world succumbed to what it originally viewed as an insignificant and ill-educated Jewish sect, embracing the otherworldly wisdom that praised the lowly poor and condemned the arrogant proud. It takes far longer for the proud to develop the pure and humble hearts that can alone welcome the heart of God.

The early Church was full of such people, not because they were necessarily born pure and humble of heart, but for another reason. When they became Christians, they embraced a way of life that would gradually allow them to become ever more docile to the Holy Spirit in whose name they were baptised. This docility enabled 'he who is mighty' to do great things in them and through them for the sake of the world that so needed the One who alone makes all things new.

The first Church grew slowly but steadily. The Christian Way required two years of preparation: learning and praying, meditating, and practising penance and charity before Baptism. After Baptism, a person's spiritual endeavours would be redoubled thanks to the graces they received. This profound and mystical journey to which they committed themselves generated a quality of love that enabled these first believers to suffer terrible imprisonment, torture, and death for the faith we easily take for granted. Furthermore, they bore the unbearable in such a way (often accompanied by astounding miracles) that torturers, executioners, and voyeurs who had attended their agonising ordeals for entertainment were moved to join them. This astonishing influence inspired Tertullian to write those famous words: 'The blood of the martyrs became the seeds of the Church'.

CHAPTER 2

To Contemplate and Share Its Fruits with Others

EVEN IN THEIR HUMDRUM DAILY LIVES, spurred on by such great saints as St John, the first Christians displayed a quality of otherworldly loving that had never been seen before. St Jerome tells us that when he was too old to walk, St John, 'the Beloved Disciple', would be carried from one Eucharistic community to another, endlessly begging his listeners to love one another as Christ commanded them to do. Remember, at the Last Supper, Christ gave them the measure that should characterise this love of others: 'You must love them as I have loved you'.

And so, they began to come in groups of hundreds and thousands, yearning to sit at the Eucharistic table to receive the same sacred food and drink Jesus had shared with his disciples at the Last Supper. They believed that with Christ in them, strengthening and supporting them from within, this love would also consume them. Such love would work for their own spiritual benefit, the Christian community's benefit, and for the world that Christ now proposed to redeem through them.

Compared with the spirituality (or rather, the spiritualities) on offer today, the God-given spirituality Christ introduced into the early Church was so simple. No wonder anyone could easily understand it and live it in union with Christ and, therefore, in union with one another in him! Sadly, Catholic lay persons today have chosen their own spirituality from a massive market of varying spiritual goodies picked and mixed at will. One likes this monastic religious order to whom they wish to affiliate themselves, and another likes this mendicant religious order; others favour the more modern congregations founded after the rise of Humanism. Still, others take a bit from all of them and then salt and pepper them with a collected variety of favourite devotions, spiritual exercises, and pious practices. Finding two Catholics today who share the same spirituality is virtually impossible. What was once so simple has now become complex, with many Catholics designing their own unique spiritual patchwork quilt of beliefs.

In the early Church, everything was simpler in preparation for their Baptism. When Christians rose from the baptismal water, called 'the womb of the Church', they were to be signed with the oil of Chrism. This anointing showed that they had now been born again and into Christ to share in his calling as the Prophet, the Priest and the King long since promised by the Prophets of old. Then, they were not clothed in a complex patchwork quilt of different, divergent, and dissimilar spiritual practices. Rather, they were draped in a single simple white garment, the same type that Christ wore when he rose from the dead on the first Easter day. This plain garment declared to the 'neophyte' that their spirituality was simple because it was simply to do but one thing: to love God in, with, and through Christ, their Risen Lord, with a pure and humble heart.

Then, for the first time, they were led in procession with those reborn again into Christ to the Eucharistic table, where they offered themselves to God as they would do each Sunday with the whole Christian community. They would offer themselves to God like never before because now they offered themselves, in, with, and through Christ to the God who created them, to be united with him to eternity. Furthermore, they were called for others just like

Christ before them. The sacred food and drink enabled them to be strengthened and supported by Christ himself as they returned to do firstly in their own family what they were called to do in the wider world.

Once the love of the Christ whom they had never seen had been generated in a new form of prayer called *meditation*, this very love enabled them to rise from meditating on the Christ who once lived on earth to enter into the Christ as he is now in heaven. Such meditation enabled them to participate in his mystical loving, his Mystical Contemplation of the Father, and also to receive the mystical love of the Father in return. His love reaches down into us like a single shaft of light; like light, it contains a multiplicity of different colours and light forms. God's light and love contain all the infused virtues and the gifts and fruits of the Holy Spirit once perfectly embodied in the Christ we are now called to represent on earth.

Let us be clear that our true vocation on earth, which is firstly to seek personal renewal and then to communicate it to others, is not fulfilled by trying to Christianise the Stoicism that has seeped into many Catholic spiritualities after the rise of Humanism. It is fulfilled by trying to do something central to the very essence of all authentic Catholic Spirituality from the beginning. That something, in the words of the great Dominican theologian St Thomas Aquinas, is 'To contemplate and then to share the fruits of contemplation with others. In a nutshell, this is the essence of the God-given spirituality first practised by Christ before introducing it to the early Church. Long may we return to it!

CHAPTER 3

A Family-Based Religion

THIS EARLY CHRISTIAN CHURCH was family-based, like the Jewish faith that preceded it. And like Jewish spirituality, it too was God-centred. Before Christ came, God seemed distant and inaccessible, whereas, in, with, and through Christ, he suddenly became near and accessible. We are told that the spirituality to which we must return is so simple because it consists of the daily observance of not one but two commandments embodied in Christ while he was on earth. First, we must love God with our whole heart and mind, with our body, and with our soul, and our whole strength, and second, we must love others, beginning at home with the selfsame love with which Christ loved others whilst he was on earth.

The first commandment would be practised in prayer at least five or six times daily, as Jesus and his disciples would have done. Firstly, at home and then secondly, in the synagogue at the third, sixth, and ninth hour when they were taught a new form of meditation in addition to the prayers that were said. This meditation enabled them to love Christ so that, like all love, they could be led on to enter into union with him and with his contemplation of God the Father. It is called the first commandment because, in the God-given spirituality that Christ has given us, it is what he himself called 'the one thing necessary'. The supernatural gifts given through God's grace in daily practising the 'one thing necessary' enabled believers to love their neighbour as Christ loves them, beginning at home in the family.

Let me describe this spirituality as it was practised by the Apostle St Paul. Immediately after he was baptised, he realised that he had been united with Christ, both symbolically and really. However, he saw immediately that this real union with Christ was initially superficial compared to the close union to which he aspired. Thus, he went into solitude where, in prayer and fasting, he could deepen his love of Christ and the union to which he aspired. As he knew he could not attain such an intimate union instantly, he went into the desert as St John the Baptist did before him to spend three years in prayer, followed by seven more years in his 'novitiate' hometown of Tarsus.

It was only then, at the insistence of St Barnabas, that he began to lead and guide others. We know what happened in his solitude, for he underwent a deep mystical purification that prepared him to do what would have been quite impossible without it. We understand this from what he said in his second letter to the Corinthians, chapter twelve. Here, he speaks of the visions and revelations he experienced fourteen years before towards the end of his 'novitiate'. He even speaks of how he was swept up into the 'third heaven', which he identified with Paradise regained.

The language associated with Mystical Theology had yet to develop. Still, any serious Mystical Theology student can recognise that St John is talking about the mystical experiences of a person who has travelled far in the 'Mystic Way'. Therefore, he had already undergone a deep and long-lasting mystical purification, which resides at the heart of the Mystic Way, where a person is prepared to be united more and more deeply with Christ and with his Mystical Contemplation of the Father, which enabled him to receive the fruits of contemplation—the love, the wisdom, the understanding, the

22

patience and all the other gifts of the Holy Spirit that can be seen throughout all his writings. How can the Holy Spirit communicate such inspired wisdom except through those whom he has purified in the Mystic Way for that very purpose?

That is why we also know that in their 'novitiate' during their retreat at Jerusalem, the other Apostles underwent this same profound inner purification that enabled the Holy Spirit to inspire them not just to preach, teach, and then write such inspired words but to die for the One who taught them. Sadly, the vast majority in our current me-me society are busily employed in searching out the latest DIY spiritualties promising instant personal self-perfection. Sometimes, those with the best will in the world but only half knowledge do the most harm because they can more easily deceive or muddle those seeking the truth.

This is particularly true of those purporting to teach Mystical Theology. Such can be seen when an attempt is made to merge contradictory spiritualities, like Carmelite and Ignatian spirituality. The first is clearly theocentric like all the older orders and supports the practice of Mystical Theology, whilst the second clearly discourages it. Like St Paul and the apostles, newcomers who rightly see the necessity of Mystical Theology should withdraw to practise it for many years before setting themselves up to lead others.

If you could separate each individual practice and belief characterising the spirituality of modern Catholics, you would find that the vast majority of them are totally orthodox. Regardless, they can be diverted from the simple way of love and from carrying their cross in the Mystic Way, where they will be purified to be united more quickly with their beloved Saviour. However, certain religious practices like the Rosary, the Stations of the Cross, and devotions (to the Sacred Heart, for instance) are unique. They are unique because, although they were introduced later, they perfectly embody within them, in an easily accessible way, the essence of the ancient Catholic spirituality.

After studying Mystical Theology and the Catholic Mystical tradition for over sixty years, I have come across hundreds of good Catholics, who, if they only knew it, had, after first fervour, been led into the beginning of the Mystic Way. However, because of the terrible spiritual ignorance of those who should know better, thanks to the historical reasons I will detail, they are sheep without shepherds. They have sadly filled the gap that their hearts yearn for with a multiplicity of questionable spiritual goodies and traditional spiritualities often at variance with each other. They can spend a lifetime going around in circles, getting nowhere, instead of following the simple way of love and love purified in the Night that leads to Eternal Life, beginning, as St John insists, in this life.

They can also muddle other Christians who find the different spiritual patchwork quilts that Catholics have made for themselves at odds with what they intuitively feel is at variance with the early Christian spirituality they encounter in their Bibles. Yet, most Catholics today who seek to live a deeper spiritual life, view the potpourri of spiritual goodies that they have chosen from the pick and mix spiritual practices on offer to be the very badge of their traditional Catholicism.

To attain genuine traditional Catholicism, we must follow the example of St John Henry Newman and go back to our origins. There, we will find the spirituality in all its simplicity that God himself gave; a spirituality first lived by Jesus Christ, who practised it, taught it to his first disciples, and then introduced it to the early Church through them. It is not my spirituality, but the spirituality practised by all the great saints and mystics throughout the ages before tragic historical events (which I am about to relate) robbed us of our spiritual birthright.

In these terrible, confusing, and frightening times when heresies are buzzing around us like hornets, and Armageddon is only a pressed button away, we must go back to the simple family-based spirituality that served our spiritual forebears so well and changed the world that they lived in beyond recognition. It transformed it from the same sort of me-me-centred world that we live in today to the God-centred world that Christ came to introduce, to redeem it by saving it from itself.

CHAPTER 4

The Unconditional Love of God

IN ORDER TO FOLLOW CHRIST from the inside we must delve deeper into the Morning Offering he made several times daily. According to Jewish custom, this prayer called the '*Shema*', was offered at least three times a day in the synagogue to coincide with the offerings made in the Temple at Jerusalem. Although Mary and Joseph and Our Lord's disciples made offerings in the Temple, there is no evidence that Jesus did the same. Why? Because he had come to introduce a new and more spiritual form of sacrifice. When talking to a Samaritan Woman, he referred to a 'New Worship in Spirit and in Truth'.

In other words, in the future, he no longer wanted people to offer physical offerings of livestock or homemade produce; rather, he wanted them to offer themselves, their whole being, embodied in their human love. This human love would finally be made fully acceptable to God because it would be made in, with, and through his human love, transformed by divine love. At last, the deepest desires of human beings from time immemorial could be made possible, thanks to the love unleashed on the first Pentecost day. Poor, weak human beings could indeed be united with the majestic God who created them. The nature of their love, however, would require transformation. The self-centred love that afflicts the best of us must be changed into the other-considering, sacrificial loving that can be seen in the love of Christ throughout his earthly life. The act (or the very many acts) involved in attempting this each day engenders the very essence of what came to be called the Mystic Way, the way that leads, in Christ, to being united with God.

New and *Old Testament* are phrases that are so weatherworn and overused that we easily forget their profound meaning. Their true significance would be far clearer if we used the expressions *New* and *Old Covenant* instead, which translate their original meaning far more relevantly. The Old Covenant began with God promising Abraham that he would make an agreement, or covenant, with him. In the Bible, there are two types of agreements. One is a mutual agreement that stands only if both parties to the agreement maintain the promises made. The other is another form of agreement - the agreement that God made with Abraham. It is a unilateral agreement, signified by the word *Berith*. In other words when God said he would love the forthcoming people generated from Abraham's seed, he committed himself to love them whether or not they responded to his love.

The great prophet who proclaimed God's unconditional love more than any other was Hosea. He proclaimed God's unconditional love in his words and by his own example. He never stopped loving his wife, Gomer, despite her having so many affairs that he admitted to not even knowing which of their children were his. When Christ extended God's original Covenant to the whole of Humanity, he, too, embodied the inner nature of God's unconditional love in his own personal life. He loved everyone with the same unconditional love of the Father who sent him. This love extended even to the people who not only hated him but hated him to death. The blood he shed on the Cross became the 'blood of the new covenant'—the new agreement—that he would continue loving his people to the end of time, whether or not they returned his love.

This new covenant is reaffirmed at each Mass celebration to remind us that God will never stop loving us through Jesus Christ, his only Begotten Son, who promised to remain with us to the end of time. Only the spiritually dead or dying can remain unmoved by this continual unconditional love that we see and hear endlessly reaffirmed each time we go to Mass. Here, that we hear Christ's word spoken again through the priest. This word ratifies this unconditional love and does much more. When we receive him into us—body, blood, soul and divinity—we receive the unconditional Lover himself. He comes so that those who receive him as they should be taken up into his mystical loving. Here, our love can mix, mingle, merge, and marry with his love, empowering us to respond to his unconditional loving as he desires. His abiding presence enables him to continue his redemptive work in the world through us. In this way, his new covenant—his new promise of unconditional love—can be open to all who are prepared to generate the self-same unconditional love that can alone unite us with him and through him with God the Father of us all.

Like Christ's daily life, this unconditional love involves making very many sacrifices by trying to do God's will. And God's will, once again, is that those who want to be united with him should first learn to love him with their whole mind and heart, their whole body and soul, and their whole strength. This learning begins in prayer, consecrating the day to God as Our Lady taught Christ to do. Let me make clear the inner nature of the simple, selfless, unalloyed, and unconditional prayer being asked of us throughout a lifetime of interior prayer. To do so, let me introduce you to St Angela of Foligno.

St Angela of Foligno was born in 1248, 22 years after St Francis of Assisi died. She herself died in 1309. Like St Francis, she came from a prosperous family. She was married to a wealthy merchant with whom she had several children. Until about forty years of age, she lived a carefree and easy life in comparative luxury and was, in her own words, a 'humbug.' However, after her husband and children died, she had a profound experience of the transcendent glory of God in the Church of San Francesco in Assisi that led to her conversion. She was then inspired to found a religious congregation committed to following the example of St Francis of Assisi, accepting his rule for his third order. Now it was St Angela who first called prayer the *Schola Divini Amoris*. In plain English, this means the School of Divine Loving. But lest you fail to understand the precise meaning of this phrase (as I did for years to the great disadvantage of my spiritual journey), let me present this as clearly as possible. It means that prayer is where you learn how to love God the same way he loves us. It is how he has always loved us and will continue to love us to the end of time and, thereafter, to all eternity, despite receiving essentially nothing from us in return.

In other words, Divine Loving encompasses the loving by which God loves us—the total, unconditional loving in which he receives little, if anything, in return from the vast majority of us. This is the loving we are invited to practise, which can ultimately unite us to God's loving because it is similar in nature to the love with which God loves us. Unless, therefore, we can come to learn this form of loving, we can never be united firstly with Christ and then in, with, and through him with God. So, when we begin learning how to pray in the *Schola Divini Amoris*, do not be surprised; rather, be grateful that prayer seems difficult precisely because, amidst countless distractions and temptations, we are being asked to give without receiving in return. Far from feeling like heaven on earth, prayer can feel more like a living hell, and everything within you revolts at the prospect of daily giving time to prayer of any sort. Prayer is where we learn the only form of loving that can unite us to God, precisely because only our simple, selfless, unalloyed, unconditional, loving can unite us with God's simple, selfless, unalloyed, unconditional loving, and so with himself.

Thanks to our baptism, we have been taken up into the Mystical Body of Christ, in, with, and through whom we learn a profound form of loving which sufficiently unites us, in, with, and through him with God. This prayer eventually leads us into Christ's Mystical Body as well as into his loving contemplation of the Father. Here, we receive in return what St Thomas Aquinas calls the fruits of contemplation that can alone perfectly remake and reform us into the image and likeness of Christ. Although St Angela was born almost eight centuries ago and beatified just over three centuries ago, she was canonised only ten years ago. Making provision for the canonisation of Angela of Foligno was nearly the last thing Pope Benedict did before resigning. Why? Because *Schola Divini Amoris* teaches the only sort of loving that can save the Church from the disaster seemingly set to destroy her.

I say *seemingly* because it will not succeed. Before disaster sets in, sufficient Catholics belonging to the Remnant will repent and turn back to God to save the Church and the entire world from extinction. In this prayer par excellence—through practising the same love Christ practised—we are united with him and with his love of the Father. With this love once again being practised as it was in the Ealy Early Church, all things—even the impossible—become possible.

CHAPTER 5

The Unconditional Love Mary Taught

WHEN OUR LADY APPEARED to a young Spanish girl, Conchita, who asked Mary to take her back to heaven with her, Mary replied, 'But what have you to bring with you?' She could say the same to us when we go to Mass. 'What have you brought with you?' In other words, when we go to Mass, we take with us the selfless sacrifices that we have been trying to make in as many times as we have repented during the previous week, both inside and outside of prayer. When these offerings, these "sacrifices", are presented to God, and precisely because they are offered in, with, and through the supreme sacrifice of Christ Our Lord at Mass, then we receive God's sanctifying grace in return to fill us with his love so that our daily repentance in the forthcoming week is ever more fully deepened.

A profoundly spiritual dynamic reoccurs week by week when we participate in Christ's Eucharistic sacrifice. God rewards our sacrifices with the sanctifying grace we receive at Mass; the Holy Spirit, who unites Christ with his Father, continually flows into us, generating an ongoing spiritual development. Over time, this spiritual development forms us more and more fully into the image and likeness of Jesus Christ. This is all part of God's plan to redeem us; then, through us, the world. Perhaps we can see more clearly the inner meaning of St Peter's repentance preached on the first Pentecost day and which Our Lady asked of us when she appeared to St Bernadette at Lourdes, the children at Fatima, and other authentic appearances apparitions. The speedy turning away from distractions and turning back to God in prayer is essential to our daily Catholic spirituality. Here, we learn the selfless, unconditional love required for uniting us with the selfless, unconditional love of God. Dissimilar things cannot unite, nor can persons be united unless they have generated the same form of loving.

From time immemorial, ancient alchemists have sought the Philosopher's Stone, that special solution or solid that could change base metal into gold. I have good news for those who have been searching for that special something. That special something has been found! Indeed, this is a special Someone who has been given to us, who can turn our base human efforts into gold. That special Someone is called the Holy Spirit, sent to us all on the first Pentecost day and on every subsequent day. He alone can turn our poor human endeavours into gold—the gold of pure, selfless, unconditional loving.

This sacrificial loving is the only form of love that can unite us to the gold of God's selfless, unalloyed, unconditional loving. He does this by entering into our weak, imperfect loving as we daily try to turn to God in and outside of prayer. Despite how humble, poor, or small our attempts are, if we persevere daily, these efforts increasingly open us to the action of the Holy Spirit; he transforms our sacrifices into the ultimate form of spiritual gold— that which can unite us to the gold of God's infinite loving.

Now, we can see the simplicity of the sublime sacrificial spirituality which leads to union with God and that Our Lady has given back to us in modern times. It is precisely the same spirituality practised by the first Christians on, and immediately after, the sending of the Holy Spirit on the first Pentecost day. Thanks to my dyslexia and

Our Lady of Fatima, it was the only spirituality I knew. It is what I practised at school and in the Franciscan novitiate, where I tested my vocation. In itself, and without any further embellishment, it is enough to lead any serious practitioner who relentlessly perseveres to the heights of sanctity, as it has done many times in the past. You do not have to be a Scholastic theologian before you can begin the journey. Before contemplation, we tried like Christian Stoics and failed, but with contemplation, we freely receive the love and sanctifying grace to progress on this journey.

After sixty-five years of journeying through the spiritual life, I have learnt many things that would have facilitated the speed of my spiritual advancement had I known about them from the beginning. I would now like to share more of them in the rest of this book. Do not worry if you get lost in my explanations or find them too difficult to follow. Simply follow Our Lady's simple teaching, taught in her most recent appearances. Repent, pray, sacrifice. Then, offer these sacrifices together with Christ's supreme sacrifice each time you attend Mass. Continually repeat what I have called this profound ongoing and mystical dynamic over and over again. I promise you will not go wrong with her help, your perseverance, and the Holy Spirit's guidance.

Along with my later further suggestions, this daily recurring pattern of prayer will lead you onward to help you see the way ahead that God has prepared for you as enacted by Our Lady. On that first Pentecost Day, being without sin, she was immediately taken into the sublime contemplation of God, in, with, and through her beloved Son Jesus, now risen and glorified. We can see ourselves in the Apostles, for they, too, were still beginners despite having spent over two years with Christ on earth. However, seeing what happened to Our Lady when the Holy Spirit descended upon her, we will understand what eventually happened to the Apostles and what will also happen to us.

When we have been sufficiently purified of our selfishness and have learnt to practise the selfless, unalloyed, and unconditional love that can alone unite us with Christ and through him with God, then what happened to our Mother Mary on the first Pentecost day will happen to us, too. Her Immaculate Conception meant that she was immediately united in contemplative prayer with her beloved Son Jesus, and she received fully the fruits of contemplation to share with her beloved children on earth where she remained. In her, therefore, we can see the very *raison d'être* and conclusion of our own prayer life here on earth, at least for those who persevere daily.

May God give us the help and strength to persevere long enough in selfless, unalloyed, unconditional loving to receive the fruits of contemplation together with the gifts and fruits of the Holy Spirit, to enable us to spend the rest of our lives living and working for the glory of God on earth—*Ad maiorem Dei gloriam.*

CHAPTER 6

Daily Sacrificial Loving

I HAVE OFTEN TOLD THE STORY of when Pope Benedict used the Internet for the first time, a young married couple with five children connected with him and asked about prayer. Their understandably busy daily life made them feel guilty about the prayer life that seemed to elude them. He told them to say their Morning Offering, and in trying to transpose it daily into practice each day, it would be sanctified, and so would everything they did that day. The Morning Offering would do for them what it was meant to do: consecrate each day to God. That the idea seemed new to them, or at least that it offered them something they had forgotten, seemed evident from their response.

Yet, consecrating the day to God was the foremost prayer uniting all the first Christians in the early Church. It came naturally to them because, as the vast majority were Jews, their mothers had taught them this prayer, albeit under the traditional name of the '*Shema*'. Naturally, after their baptism, they taught it to new converts because it was so important, but now with a Christian formula, with the new ending, 'in, with, and through Christ our Risen Lord'.

What appeared novel to the young Catholic couple was the norm for all in the early Church. It was learnt at their mother's knee from their earliest years or in preparation for baptism for new converts, whether Jewish or not. They would have been taught that Jesus himself said this prayer thrice daily with his disciples in the Synagogue: at nine in the morning, midday, and three in the afternoon. For the Jews of the Old Testament, this enabled those saying their *Shema* in the Synagogue to be spiritually united with the physical offerings being made in the Old Temple in Jerusalem. But, as Jesus came to introduce a deeper and more spiritual form of worship, his new followers were taught to pause at nine in the morning, midday, and three in the afternoon. This practice aimed not to enforce identifying themselves with the old worship in the Temple at Jerusalem but rather with the new worship offered by Jesus Christ on the Cross. This is the worship that Christ—the New Temple—continues to offer in heaven with all who have been reborn into him at baptism.

As Jesus explained to the Samaritan woman, this worship was a new worship 'in Spirit and in Truth'. This new worship could be seen as practised by Christ throughout his life but, most of all, in his final moments when he was being crucified to death. It was a profoundly interior, spiritual, or mystical offering because onlookers could not see it. For many, Christ's crucifixion might have seemed like just another criminal being put to death by the Roman authorities. In fact, that death had just been offered to God by Jesus in Gethsemane. Although his human nature was repulsed by what was being asked of him, he nevertheless committed himself to doing what he had always done: his Father's will. And he committed to do it to the end, to complete a lifetime in which he did everything as an offering, a living sacrifice to his Father.

This new worship was then essentially an inner spiritual sacrifice. It is the new worship in 'Spirit and in Truth' to which those who commit themselves to follow him dedicated themselves in what was originally called the *'Shema'*, and which we now call our Morning Prayer. Like the first Christians, we should remember thrice daily the most perfect Offering ever made— 'in Spirit and in Truth'— by recalling Christ's condemnation to death at nine o'clock in the morning, his crucifixion at noon, and his death on the Cross, his ultimate supreme sacrifice to his Father, at three o'clock in the afternoon.

My own father used to put three stickers on his watch to remind him to recall and give thanks for the supreme sacrifice Christ made for us. It also reminded him that by putting his morning offering into practice through everything he did each day in the way he tried to love others as Christ loved him, he would be uniting himself with Christ's redemptive action. He would be doing this for himself, and also so Christ could continue his redeeming action for the world through him. These brief daily moments when we remind ourselves of Christ's ongoing redemptive action and how we can participate in his action every day can help us do what our first Christian forebears did before us. They learnt under the ongoing inspiration and influence of the Holy Spirit to practise this new worship in spirit and truth, even when it meant giving their lives for Christ in physical martyrdom.

When this new worship did not lead to red martyrdom (physical death), Christians welcomed the opportunity to embrace white martyrdom (a sacrificial life). This non-bloody martyrdom was achieved through the daily practice of trying to unite themselves with Christ by making the daily offering in word and deed in all they said and did each day. Thus, they always began by consecrating their day to God as Jesus did before them. We have the witness of two great saints whose testimony reminds us of how this profound daily inner sacrifice, practised daily, found its liturgical expression in the Mass.

Less than a century after Christ's Sacrifice on the Cross, St Justin wrote of the supreme moment when the whole congregation together pronounced their commitment to the new spiritual sacrifice uniting them with Christ's sacrifice. Together with him, they would give all honour and glory to the One to whom they had consecrated every moment of every day of their lives. At the end of the great Eucharistic Prayer, when all was offered to God in one voice in the great doxology, the 'Amen' nearly shook the roof off the Church! Two hundred years later, and over three hundred years after Christ died for us on the Cross, St Jerome said that the sound of this great 'Amen' resounded like a thunderclap around the Basilica in which Christ's supreme act of redemptive sacrifice was being celebrated.

This Amen that they all said as one was the definitive acclamation that decisively ratified the very essence of the profound sacrificial spirituality lived by the early Christians in imitation of their Lord and Master, Jesus Christ. It was the outward manifestation of the simple but exacting sacrificial spirituality that led onward into union with Christ, their Risen Lord. Then in, with, and through him, to contemplate God himself, sometimes in darkness, sometimes in light. And finally, in the very act of doing this, to receive the fruits of contemplation for themselves and for the world Christ chose to redeem through them.

Reform (or *renewal* or *rebirth*) means returning to this simple (though I do not say *easy*) Christ-given Spirituality. Imagine what would happen if all the Remnant said their morning offering in unison with one another each day and together tried to put it into practice, in, with, and through Christ. If it did not transform the modern world into a Christian world, as our first forebears did for the ancient pagan world, then many of our old churches would need new roofs, as congregations give vent to their joy at returning to the practice of a religion once so loved but recently so forgotten.

CHAPTER 7

Personal Sanctification and Redemption

THERE ARE TWO MAIN PILLARS of Catholic Spirituality. Both involve selfless, unconditional, sacrificial loving. Firstly, there is the selfless, unconditional, sacrificial loving of Jesus Christ that began when he was born, and which reached its summit on the Cross. This sacrificial loving is made present in the Mass. The second pillar of Catholic Sacrificial Spirituality is the selfless, unconditional, sacrificial loving we try to practise in imitation of Christ's selfless, sacrificial loving. The spiritual strength to do this is given in the graces of Baptism and whenever we go to Mass. It comes from the fullness of Grace that the Greek Fathers called the *Pleroma*, that poured into Christ as, in the words of St John, he was glorified by God at the moment of his death on the Cross.

At Mass, when Christ becomes present, he is present for us at the moment of his glorification when the fruits of his lifelong unconditional sacrifice are pouring into us to give us the spiritual strength to take up our daily cross and to initiate the selfless, sacrificial, and unconditional love that was the hallmark of every moment of his life on earth. However, this love can be given and received only by those who come to Mass bearing sacrifices to offer, made since they last came to Mass. If we come bearing nothing, then we receive nothing; the Mass is therefore meaningless, not in itself, of course, but for those who come empty-handed. You may put $1,000 in the plate, but it will do you no good without the sacrifices God wants you to give from your heart. Lest there be any misunderstanding, the sacrifices he desires are acts of self-denial in the time granted to loving God in prayer. It is the selfless, sacrificial loving practised in prayer and offered in the sacrifices made to love God in the neighbour in need and to act like Christ in all we say and do.

These little sacrifices may seem like matchwood crosses compared to the Cross Christ carried, but they are the beginning of a journey in which his loving and your loving become one. The sacrificial loving Christ practised came to be called Redemptive Loving because it redeems us from the devil and all his devices to imprison us in sinfulness and self-absorption. As slaves could be redeemed by money, Christ has redeemed us by his love, symbolised by the blood he shed to the last drop on the Cross. When St John tells us that he actually saw that last drop of blood shed for us as he stood with Our Lady at the foot of the Cross, he also saw the water that followed it. This symbolised the outpouring of God's love to be received by those who would follow him, making possible what is quite impossible without it.

When we put our Morning Offering into practice each day through daily sacrifices, we are taking part in the redemptive action of Our Lord Jesus Christ, as his love begins the work of our redemption. As we, in our turn, share with others what he is doing for us, we are participating in his redemptive action for the world, which he chooses to redeem through us. All the daily sacrifices we make enabling us to imitate him make us one with him and with the Father who sent him, simultaneously involving us personally in the redemption of the world as God planned from the beginning.

Consequently, in saying our Morning Offering, our Christian *Shema,* and putting it into practice, we cooperate with God who created us. In our daily prayer, in trying to put the offering that we make there into practice in our daily lives, we are practising the selfless, unconditional loving that Christ himself practised throughout his earthly life. For in the *Shema* taught by his mother, the first commandment to love God with your mind and heart, with your body and soul, and with your whole strength has been transposed into a prayer.

If we follow his example in our morning prayer, then we can do the same in, with, and through him. This will then enable us to practise the two new commandments of the New Covenant that Jesus himself gave us: firstly, to love God with our whole mind and heart, with our body and soul and with our whole strength; and secondly, to love our neighbour as Christ loves us. Christ's promise at the Last Supper will be fulfilled as we try to do this. For those who strive to keep his commandments, he will send the Holy Spirit to be with us and, even more, to be within us. Then, he said he would come with the Father to make his home in us. Once we are filled with his love, all things that are impossible without him will be possible. We will enable him to work in and through us to bring about the salvation, the sanctification, and the redemption of the world, beginning with ourselves.

Prayer: God, our Father, I want to consecrate the forthcoming day to you by loving you with my whole mind and heart, with my body and soul, and with my whole strength in all that I say and do. I wish to do this in this forthcoming day, just as Jesus did every day of his life on earth. Please accept what I do so imperfectly and unite it with the perfect offering that Jesus continues to make to you in heaven and on earth each time Holy Mass is celebrated. I offer to you my joys and my sorrows, my successes as well as my failures, because these especially show how much I have need of you. I make my prayer in, with, and through Jesus, in whom we all live and move and have our being. Amen.

CHAPTER 8

One Thing to Change the World

WHEN AN ANCIENT SAGE WAS ASKED if he could do just one thing to change the world for the better, he said he would give back to words their true meaning. Unfortunately, I cannot do that, but I would like to give back to just one word its true meaning because our life, our happiness, and our ultimate destiny depend more on this word than on any other. The word is *Love*. Life without love is meaningless.

The very essence of the God-given Spirituality Jesus bequeathed to the early Church can be summed up in this simple word: Love. Not our love, but God's love, as St John insisted. This love that Jesus received in its fullness when he was glorified is continually pouring out of him. Prayer—deep prayer—is the word we use to describe what we must do to turn and open our hearts to receive this love.

This deep prayer existed before, but Jesus gave it a new meaning and power that it never had before and a new name, too. It came to be called Mystical Prayer. As we have seen, the word *mystical* comes from Greek, meaning *unseen, invisible, or secret*. Christ taught this new type of Mystical Prayer to his first followers, for it was the prayer he himself used to communicate with his Father. In the Jewish religion in which he grew up, prayer was predominantly audible. This evident prayer inevitably led to some hypocrisy that Christ did not want his followers to fall into, so he advised them accordingly. 'When you pray', he told them, 'go into your private room and when you have closed the door, pray to your Father who is in that secret place, and your father who sees all that is done in secret will reward you' (Matthew 6:6).

Later, this secret, unseen, invisible Mystical Prayer was given a totally new dimension and power. This happened when all who received the Holy Spirit after the first Pentecost were drawn up and into the Mystical Body of Christ, where they, too, would reside in future. They would pray in, with, and through him to the Father, who would reward them as Jesus had promised.

Although I spent many years reading books on spiritual theology, I came to understand the Mystic Way's true meaning from my parents. After my mother died, my father told me that in the last years of their married life together, he and my mother loved each other more deeply and more perfectly than at any other time in their lives. In the first days of what he described as their adolescent love, they were drawn to each other by powerful waves of emotional and passionate feelings that he could never forget. They acted like the boosters on a spaceship, raising it off the ground on its way to outer space. Just as these powerful boosters fizzle out, so do the powerful boosters of adolescent love in every marriage.

My father explained to me that it was what happened between the moment when these powerful emotional feelings fizzled out, and the perfect love that was experienced at the end of their lives, that made this perfect love possible. For many years, no decades, unknown to onlookers, unseen even to their closest friends and relatives, they practised selfless, sacrificial, Mystical Loving, whether they felt like it or whether they did not—come hell or high water. This totally other-considering, Mystical Loving gradually enabled

43

them to bond ever closer together until, in their last years together, they enjoyed as perfect a union as is possible in this life.

Families were made by Love in the first place. They were made for love and to propagate love above all else. Therefore, I will be writing about this teaching of Mystical Theology. This teaching alone can teach us to do and continually sustain us in doing what Christ himself called 'the one thing necessary'. This 'one thing necessary' is the prayer that can alone bring about our own personal sanctification, the sanctification of the Church, and the sanctification of the world for which Christ founded his Church. For even the love of God needs our freely given love in return to receive it.

Prayer is simply the word we use to describe the way in which our intimate personal loving is directed to God by being taken up into His Mystical Contemplation of his Father to receive what only he can give in return. Consequently, St Teresa of Avila said, 'There is only one way to perfection and that is to pray. If anyone points you in another direction, then they are deceiving you'. But now we must move on to see and understand the ultimate nature of the only love that can save us and, through us, redeem the world. This attempt at understanding will involve a certain amount of repetition as I summarize the teaching I have already explained in my earlier books and blogs, podcasts, and video lectures that I have given in the past. However, it will enable us to go forward into a fuller and more complete understanding of the only love that can transform and transfigure us into the image and likeness of the man we have committed ourselves to follow.

CHAPTER 9

Back to the Future

EVERYONE HAS A BEE IN THEIR BONNET. Fr Tetlow, an English diocesan priest who taught me classics at school, had one bee in his bonnet that would sting him at least once a term as he was teaching us Greek and ancient history. 'Gentlemen', he would say, 'everyone can criticise; it is the easiest thing in the world to do. If you do have to criticise, make it positive, constructive, and based on the truth, not as you see it but as it is. It is easy to criticise the contemporary Church. Anyone can and is doing it, but genuine, positive, and constructive criticism is another matter. This can only come by comparing the failings we see in the contemporary Church and some of the bizarre, if not heretical, ways that contemporary 'modernists' want to 'reform' the Church with the truth. The truth is the God-given teaching Christ introduced into the early Church through the apostles.

There are, for instance, many different spiritualities in the Church that have developed over time. However, they are only good as far as they reproduce the one and only God-given spirituality that Christ introduced into early Christianity. All later spiritualities only reproduce this spirituality for different people, in different circumstances, and in different ways of life. If such spiritualities deviate substantially from what is the perfect paradigm found in its original purity in Apostolic times, then they should be abandoned.

Whenever these later spiritualities set about renewing themselves, the sign of their authenticity will always be the way in which they return to the sources that originally inspired them. Benedictines, for instance, derive their original inspiration from the faithful community in Jerusalem formed immediately after the Resurrection. Dominicans find their inspiration from the apostolic way of life as lived by the first apostles. Franciscans base their way of life on the life as lived by Jesus and his disciples.

I have detailed the divine origins of primitive Christian spirituality in the first twelve chapters of my book, *Wisdom from The Christian Mystics – How to Pray the Christian Way*. I have done this there and elsewhere and will continue to do so because so-called 'new spiritualities' are presently raising their heads within the Catholic Church as I write. Many totally contradict Christ's teaching, which was as essential to the early Catholic Church, even as it still is today, as a spirituality that was inspired and introduced by Our Divine Lord himself cannot be challenged. Some modern heretics carry an agenda of subtly reintroducing Arianism. They argue, as the Arians did, that if Christ is no more than just a man, albeit the greatest man who ever lived, then this would make a big difference. Why? Because then they would argue that he would see that what was right for the Church two thousand years ago would not be right for the Church today. In short, he would be introducing new modern agendas that 'sophisticated' modern Catholics (like us, of course) wish to introduce. This insidious infiltration of Catholicism has already begun in the Church from top to bottom. Whilst not openly proclaiming that Christ was only a man, they simply mention him less and less while mentioning themselves and their worldly-wise ways more and more. These preposterous suggestions of renewal are aeons away from the God-given spirituality that Christ introduced into the early Church.

There are clearly two contradictory trends or movements in the

Church today. The first trend turns to tradition to change the world, and the second turns to the world to change tradition. The first is theocentric; the second is anthropocentric. The God-given spirituality introduced into the early Church by Christ that is the subject of this book comes a poor second to the man-made 'spiritualities' that have been cherry-picked and implemented by amateurs from the latest human fads and fashions, such as the psychosociological sciences that many have turned to instead of to Christ for personal redemption. These false spiritualities were no more than a passing fad for some, but they have had a devastating effect for others.

The anti-contemplative ethos and invective that inspired these reformers has spread like an underground fungus. It has mushroomed in an unprecedented manner with the encouragement and active support of some of the Church's highest authorities. It would seem they are bent on extinguishing what Pope St John Paul II called the very soul of the Church——its contemplative life—to make way for the latest 'here today and gone tomorrow' anthropocentric fashions. Although Henry VIII destroyed the monasteries, he did not, nor could he, destroy their mystical life, for so many of the monks, friars, and religious women fled to the European continent to continue their contemplative life there. But it seems that many Church authorities today are trying to extinguish at its source the heart and soul of contemplative prayer, which is, as it always has been, the lifeblood of those united in the Mystical Body of Christ.

Like Judaism, from which it derived, Christianity was primarily a domestic spirituality in which the family was paramount. Why not, therefore, go back to discover what can immediately be applied to our lives? This rediscovery would serve us better than trying to understand and live it through the spirituality of a religious order that was not primarily founded for lay people living in the world. We can still be inspired by religious orders and look to them for help and guidance in our prayer life and our spiritual search for God.

Yet, we are the ones responsible for applying the principles of our faith and learning how we sanctify our lives as our first Christian ancestors did.

The first Christians practised what they called 'white martyrdom' and 'carrying their daily Cross' so that their whole lives became like the Mass. Every action—in and through all that they said and did—became a continual offering of themselves through Christ to God. Through which all they said and did, we can learn to do the same in our own day to day lives. This perpetual offering was the new worship 'in spirit and in truth' that Christ promised to the Samaritan woman and introduced into the early Church, as it had been practised in Christ's own daily life. What was primarily done for the Church in later centuries under the influence and inspiration of religious orders was done in the first Christian centuries by lay people inspired and animated from within by the dynamic action of the Holy Spirit.

Today, we are facing one of the greatest crises ever in the history of the Church, and there seems little if any, evidence to show that those who came to the rescue before are poised to save us from impending disaster. Tragically, fewer and fewer religious orders exist, and they are sadly weaker and weaker than they once were since abandoning their contemplative origins. It is time for the domestic Church to rise and do what it did for the Church in the first Christian centuries. That is why I am primarily writing for lay Catholics and detailing the same spirituality that inspired and sustained those first Christian families in the early Church. If we cannot see that the family is at present the last bastion against the Church's own destruction, then I can assure you that her enemies have. For this reason, the Church's enemies are presently launching the most fierce and vicious attack on the family ever known in the history of the Church or even in the history of humanity.

Here, in the domestic Church, we must rally together and mutually support one another before trying to do for the modern pagan world what the first Christian families did for the ancient pagan world. This transformation needs totally committed lay people prepared to abandon themselves daily to the Holy Spirit in an ever-deepening prayer life. Only the development of an ever-deepening prayer life will enable you to become ever more porous to the Holy Spirit, who will do through you what is quite impossible without him.

CHAPTER 10

Lay Spirituality

FR GABRIEL REIDY OFM WAS THE MOST ERUDITE MAN I have ever met. His advice set me back on the right path for the rest of my life. Later, in an oral examination, he asked me whether lay spirituality was originally monastic or mendicant spirituality that had filtered down to the laity or was it a religious spirituality in its own right. In short, did it derive from the spirituality lived in monasteries, priories or friaries, or did it have a different origin all its own? I answered that lay spirituality originated in the spirituality lived by those who took vows and lived in religious communities that filtered down to the laity. He was such a gentleman that he did not say that I was wrong; he just said that he held the other theory, relegating my empty-headed guess to a theory! In the book he was writing on lay spirituality, he insisted that lay people looking for a spirituality on which to base their lives should look no further than the God-given spirituality that Our Lord introduced into the early Church.

Although the later spiritualities of those who chose a celibate life may inspire us, and their teaching on prayer and other principles of the spiritual life may help us, we must firstly look to the spirituality that Christ gave to the laity in the early Church. The point Fr Gabriel was trying to make was that rather than being encouraged to become semi-detached members of later spiritualities designed for celibates. The laity should be encouraged to return to this profound spirituality. Although I will be spending a great deal of time detailing the unique teaching on prayer of the great Carmelite Doctors of the Church, St John of the Cross and St Teresa of Avila, I have not tried to base my own daily spiritual life on the way in which they lived their semi-monastic life within their religious communities. Instead, I have tried to base my daily spiritual timetable around the way in which Jesus lived with his first disciples and how it continued to develop, most particularly for and by lay people and their families in those first Christian centuries. What was primarily done for the Church in later centuries under the influence and inspiration of religious orders was done in the first Christian centuries by lay people, inspired and animated from within by the dynamic action of the Holy Spirit.

This spirituality was primarily given to and lived by ordinary families long before religious life as we know it came into being. It is available to all and can be found in the scriptures, the writings of the Fathers of the Church, and in the works of great modern writers like Fr Joseph Jungman SJ as well as many others. In essence, this family-based spirituality had already been lived by Christ himself. For he was filled with the human love of his earthly father and mother and simultaneously filled with the divine love of his heavenly Father. He wanted this same love that totally transformed him to be available to all. That is why he sent the Holy Spirit on the first Pentecost day to make many more Holy Families in which human loving was surcharged by Divine Loving as his had been.

These families would become the spiritual powerhouses from which the ancient pagan world would be converted. This transformation would happen not so much because of the message they would preach but more so by the supernatural quality of the unprecedented love animating them and their families. Long before religious life developed in the guise of Monasticism, thanks to St Antony

(AD 252-356), Christian Spirituality was predominantly devised for and lived by lay Christians. Religious life as we know it today did not exist. That the Mass and the sacraments were administered by a predominantly married clergy in the early Church was to be expected since Christianity was part of the natural evolution from the Jewish family-based religion.

However, the spiritual reasons why celibate clergy gradually became the norm are as valid today as in the past. Therefore, a return to married clergy as the norm plays no part in the suggestions for renewal put forward in this book. Nor is my emphasis on lay spirituality intended to undermine or disempower the hierarchical structure of the Church set in place from the beginning but rather to re-empower its authority, deriving from tradition and thriving on holiness.

Since the Church became over-clericalized after the ascendancy of Constantine and a newfound freedom for Christians led to laxity, the central role of lay spirituality in the Church was gradually undermined. Furthermore, when the Roman Emperor, Theodosius the Great (AD 379-395), proclaimed that henceforth Christianity would be the official religion of his Empire, this state of affairs gradually worsened, as liberty led to laxity. It would no longer be predominantly the family but rather senior celibate clerics and religious orders who would take pride of place. I will return to this theme later. However, I will tell you the imminent conclusion now so that there need be no delay in presenting you the opportunity to return to the Spirituality first lived by Christ and then, through his Apostles, given to the early Church.

The conclusion is very simple, for it depends on love. Not our love but God's love, for that love and that love alone can transform us and our families and, through them, the whole world. But if we choose not to learn to practise the prayer which opens us to receive God's love, then nothing will happen.

CHAPTER 11

With Love All Things Are Possible

WHEN BILL HALEY & HIS COMETS introduced Rock and Roll into Britain in the 1950s, the older generation was terrified at what was happening to the younger generation. While most parish priests were condemning the American musical vandals and their revolutionary music, our parish priest was encouraging his youth club to revel in it. He even invited imitation groups to entertain them!

Although this made him the most popular parish priest we ever had, at least with the young, he alienated himself from others. Like most of the parish priests at the time, he continually warned against mixed marriages when they thought that love was enough. I am afraid I was one of those who thought with the Beatles that 'love, love, love is all you need'. Of course, it all depends on what you mean by *love*. Although the Beatles claimed they were more popular than Jesus Christ, Christ's idea of love was far less superficial than theirs. It was also far more exacting, far more substantial, and, therefore, far more enduring. For Christ, you demonstrate true love when preparing to give everything for those you love. When you do this, the most exciting thing you have ever experienced happens— you begin to receive their love in return.

That is why, when Jesus loved God without measure, he received God's love in return without measure. This love not only filled him with happiness but also everything else that God's love brings. It brings all the help and strength to love others with such a quality of selflessness and self-sacrificial goodness that others feel impelled to return in kind. When this sort of other-considering love is given, and given repeatedly, to that other special person whom love has inspired us to marry, then we are open to enjoy the mutual loving that will overflow onto and into our families. This loving that makes the human family on earth the finite sign and exemplification of the infinite divine family in heaven—our final destiny. Therefore, this loving proved to be the primary and magnetic force drawing and inspiring those who belonged to ancient pagan religions to join the new Christian religion. Here, they could see and experience the love that animated Christian families. They wished to animate their families, too!

For this reason, Christ called upon all who would follow him to do what he did every moment of every day of his life. Namely, to observe the first and most important of God's commandments, to love God with your whole heart and mind, with your whole body and soul, and with your whole strength. To do this and receive his love in return, they were taught how they must be emptied of all other loves and desires preventing them from receiving his love. One of the Desert Fathers once told his followers that if they wished to draw sufficient water from the well, they would have to empty their buckets from everything else. In the same way, they were told that their hearts would have to be emptied of all other loves and desires if their hearts were to be filled with Christ's love, enabling them to be united with his Father through him.

Consequently, the two years of preparation required of all would-be Christians for baptism were filled with prayer, penance, and good works. This preparatory asceticism enabled them to be better prepared to be taken up into Christ's Mystical Body once they were baptised. However, that would not be the end but the beginning of their journey into God. For within his Mystical Body, this daily asceticism must continue in order to be united not only with his Mystical Body but also with his mystical heart that is forever loving God. The more the two hearts become one, the more they act together, pray together and love together. And the more perfectly can they share in Christ's own contemplation of his Father.

In studying the spirituality of the early Church, I gradually came to understand my parish priest's point of view. Of course, it would be wrong to dismiss 'mixed marriages' out of hand. However, if Catholic families had taught their children how to practise the self-denial, the self-sacrifice, and the daily prayer that would open them to the love of God, then what they gave and what they received in their spiritual lives would guarantee them a far greater chance of living life-long, loving marriages. And if both members of the married couples had the same spiritual upbringing, then this chance would be far further advanced. This shared spirituality would enable these families to become in today's world what they were in the ancient world—the main dynamic force swiftly converting a pagan Empire into a Christian Empire.

I agree with all other writers, columnists and critics who rightly draw our attention to the unprecedented moral mess in which our world and our Church is entangled and many of the solutions deemed necessary to remedy the disarray. However, I am concentrating on what is needed to achieve the disentanglement. For without the transformation of hearts that Christ came to bring, we will never be able to realise the noble ideals we want to accomplish. *Prayer* is the word used to describe what we must do to open our hearts to the only One who can transform and animate them with love. Once again, therefore, may I introduce you to the personal prayer taught for generations by saints and mystics from the beginning. I have collected these for you in podcast form on my website and the website of Essentialist Press. For with the prayer that opens us to the love of God, all things are possible that are quite impossible without it.

CHAPTER 12

Is Anybody Listening?

EVERY MONDAY AFTERNOON AT 4.30 PM, BBC Radio 4 runs a programme called 'Beyond Belief'. Last week, the wife of a Jewish Rabbi said that every day, she reads a page of the Talmud. The Talmud is an ancient Jewish book that details the everyday customs and prayers that are practised by devout Jews. When the Romans destroyed Jerusalem in AD 70 and the Jewish people were forced to find new homes all over the Roman Empire, it was feared that their beloved religion with all its prayers and customs would be lost. It was for this reason that scribes and Rabbis began to collect them together for posterity in the book that came to be called the *Talmud*. Reading this book gives us an insight into the practical spirituality of the Jews at the time when Jesus was born.

More precisely, we are given an insight into the daily devotional prayers and practices of the Holy Family that Mary and Joseph taught to their son, Jesus, as he was growing up. All of a sudden, you find that the so-called 'hidden years' are not so hidden, as we have been led to believe, at least in what really matters—the personal spiritual life that formed Our Lord. Why, then, are they not detailed in our New Testament? The answer is that all the first Christians were Jews who, to begin with, carried on practising the customs and prayers they were taught since childhood by their Jewish parents. Therefore, why bother detailing what everybody knew and practised? Why tell everyone to do what they were already doing? All the writers of the New Testament practised the prayer life that was their heritage, and they assumed (and assumed correctly) that their readers were doing the same. Consequently, they did not keep referring to them.

If you love good food, you will undoubtedly be a devotee of Delia Smith, Mary Berry, Nigella Lawson, Gary Rhodes, Rick Stein, or some other master chef. Whether you read their books, listen to their radio programmes, or watch their television shows, they all make an understandable assumption about their followers. They all assume the people in their audience have time to cook, know how to cook, and have a place where they can cook—namely, a kitchen. It was the same with the first Christian teachers. They all assumed their followers had the time to love, the knowledge of how to love, and a place to love—namely, personal prayer. What the culinary teachers want to teach is their philosophy of food, how to produce it, present it, and share it with others, beginning with your own family. In the same way, what the first Christian teachers wanted to teach was their theology of love, how to produce it, present it, and how to share it with others, beginning with their own families.

When you read the writings of the New Testament and the Church Fathers, you will read about the God-given theology of love Christ introduced into the early Church. You will also read how to put this teaching into practice in the exemplary moral life you must live at all times. But you will not read about the daily life of Mystical Prayer they presumed everybody was practising, precisely because it is assumed, and rightly so. However—and this is crucial—without the love of God received in this Mystical Prayer that will suffuse and surcharge weak and feckless human loving, we will never have the wisdom to see the God-given theology Christ introduced into the early Church. Furthermore, without it, we will certainly never live the high moral life that it demands of us in the world in which we live.

By *Mystical Prayer,* I mean the daily, invisible, personal prayer that could not be seen. It was hidden not just because it took place inside their hearts but because it took place inside the invisible or Mystical Body of Christ. Here, through mystical purification, their hearts would be united ever more completely with the heart of Christ to share in his Mystical Contemplation of his father. What they received in return was a quality of love containing within it all the virtues enabling them to live the same sort of virtuous life Christ had lived. The same virtuous life Christ still lives because he continues to live it in, with, and through us. Modern readers of the scriptures must realise that however much their readings may enthral them and however much they may be inspired to put their moral teaching into practice in their own lives, this will not be possible without the mystical loving that must be learnt in prayer. In the past, this love was assumed because it was lived. Sadly, today, it is assumed but not lived. Hence, the moral malaise in which we are living. That is why all the great saints and mystics and now Our Lady herself keep calling people back to prayer. Is anybody listening?

This book details the profound God-given spirituality Christ introduced to the early Church, yet it is essential that I do something else. As clearly as possible, I must draw your attention to the profound Mystical Prayer underpinning it, without which it could not have been practised in the beginning, just as it cannot be lived today. Therefore, I have gathered together the teaching on Catholic Mystical Prayer from the beginning and made it available to you on my website and on the website of Essentialist Press. For the truth of the matter is, that without this prayer, you can only stand back in awe and admire the spirituality that I will describe for you, but you will never be able to live it. If there were a Catholic Talmud in which the traditional prayer of Catholic saints and mystics have been taught through the ages, I would like to think that you will find it in this book, albeit in story form, to make it as simple and as readable as possible.

CHAPTER 13

The Greatest of All Mystics

IT WAS ON THE EVE OF CHRISTMAS, many years ago, that I was told I had failed my religious knowledge examination; I cried myself to sleep. I was only ten years old at the time, and the news devastated me. It was the worst Christmas I ever had. When asked to explain what the Immaculate Conception meant, I said it meant that Our Lord was born free from all sin. When I complained to the parish priest, he explained that although what I said was totally correct, the expression *Immaculate Conception* was usually used to describe how Our Lady was conceived without sin.

Understanding the importance of Christ being conceived and born without sin is of vital importance if we are to understand the nature of our own spiritual journey. The scriptures put it this way. They insist that when he was born, he was born like us in every way except that he was born without sin (Hebrews 4:15). This meant that from the moment of his birth in a wooden crib until the moment of his death on a wooden cross, there was nothing to prevent him being at all times open to receive the love of God. What the great mystics call Mystical Contemplation and what St Thomas Aquinas describes as 'a simple vision of God accompanied by awe' was possible for some mystics for some of the time. But it was open to Our Lord for all the time he was on earth and for all eternity when he was in heaven.

Now we can see how God's plan to enable mere human beings like us to love him and for him to love us could be brought about by sending his Holy Spirit to draw us up into our Risen Lord. We are drawn not just into his Mystical Body but into his mystical loving of his Father, too. However, before the death of Jesus, his Mystical Body did not exist as it did after the Resurrection. So, when he gathered his first disciples together for prayer, they prayed with him at the same time as he did, even using the same prayers he used but not as they would in the future. For in the future, after the first Pentecost when the Holy Spirit had drawn them up into his Mystical Body, they would now begin to pray in, with, and through him in a way they had never prayed before and so more powerfully than ever before.

However, there was a clear difference between the prayer of those who had just been taken up into his Mystical Body and Jesus' prayer. The difference was this. They were not conceived without sin as he had been. Therefore, they were sinners, and so something had to happen before they could be totally at one with him and with his prayer and his Mystical Contemplation of his Father. This *something* was a profound inner mystical purification in which their hearts could be sufficiently purified to become as one with Christ's own Sacred Heart. This purification would, of course, take time because the power of Original Sin could not be destroyed without years of daily dying to self by taking up the cross and following in his footsteps.

There is no such thing as instant purification, as St Paul was to discover the hard way. Yes, he may well have had a conversion experience on the road to Damascus. Nevertheless, as Monsignor Philip Hughes shows in his monumental *A History of the Church*, St Paul had to spend ten years in prayer and penance in a self-chosen 'novitiate' before he could become the great Apostle to the Gentiles. Even then, he kept falling into sin (Romans 7:18-20). In short, before he could say, 'I live, no it is not I who live but Christ who lives in me', he, like everybody else, needed his heart to be purified before it could be sufficiently united with the heart of Christ, the prayer of Christ, and his Mystical Contemplation. This unification did finally happen, as he famously describes in his second letter to the Corinthians (12:1-5). When you begin to pray, not just with Christ but in him and with him, then you also begin to receive in return the love Our Lord received when he was on earth. Then all things become possible, even the impossible, as we can read in the Acts of the Apostles, in the Acts of the Martyrs, and in the History of the Early Church.

What can be said of St Paul can be said of the other Apostles. Even after coming to know and love Christ in his physical body during his life on earth, they too had to spend many years 'in retreat' in Jerusalem, living, praying, and breaking bread together (Acts 2:42) to be purified sufficiently to be united with Christ's prayer and with his mystical loving of his Father. For this reason, new converts would, in future, have to spend two years praying, fasting, and helping the poor before they could be baptised and then continue after baptism in the same way, preparing for the union with Christ. Unfortunately, in recent years, all too many converts to the Catholic Church have not had the many years of prayerful preparation and purification that the first Apostles all underwent.

That babies can be baptised and introduced into the family of God without doing anything to deserve it is one of the most striking examples of God's totally gratuitous gift of love. But this inestimable privilege does not mean that they should not be taught how to come to know, love, and be ever more deeply united with Christ as soon as they are able. That this has not happened in the past is tragic, but that this must be remedied in the present is imperative. Therefore, the first principle of any genuine Catholic catechetical program is to teach children facts about the faith and also how to love Jesus, who was born on the first Christmas day, so that he can be born again in them. Then, like Mary, his Mother and their mother, they can give him to the world that is lost without him.

CHAPTER 14

From Loving to Union

I WAS HARDLY OUT OF MY PRAM when World War II began. I may not have any war wounds to brag about, but I do have memories, terrible memories, of the fear that gripped me when the sirens began to whine. I would hear the planes and the rockets overhead and the sound of the bombs exploding, and I would see the incendiaries setting our houses on fire as I ran to the air raid shelter.

As our family passed the picture of the Sacred Heart in the hallway, we would all pray for spiritual strength and support and to be saved from the horrible death that may await us at any moment. It helped me realise the terrible fear that must have petrified the early Christians. Their enemies were not high up in the sky, threatening to destroy them. They were all around them, threatening to put them to death if they did not worship their gods or buy livestock to sacrifice in their temples or if they did not conform to the Roman Empire ruling over them. They even considered it an affront if Christians did not take part in their sordid games when slaves were killed for sport or in their all-night drinking parties and sexual orgies, commonplace in those days. Even when there was no official persecution, neighbours would report them to the local authorities, sending them to prison, where torture, scourging, and death were not the exception but rather the rule. I would have been far more terrified then than in the war, when at least the enemy was not on the ground, and we had a sturdy air raid shelter as well as loving parents and caring nurses and hospitals to go to if we were injured.

But, like us, the first Christians did have the same Risen Lord to turn to, who had promised to be with them to the end of time. They did not have pictures of him in their homes as we did because they still took the Second Commandment seriously and would not have any man-made images in their homes or in their churches, at least to begin with. Consequently, the first apostles and the first disciples taught the faithful to picture Christ in their minds, in their memories, and in their imaginations so that they could more easily come to know and love him as they did while he was on earth. They even taught them to imagine him as they had seen him preaching God's message of love and then dying for proclaiming it to his people. They were taught to picture his agonising death, to see in their mind's eye the length and breadth, the height and depth of his love for them. In the Resurrection, they would see God's love for his Son and the other great mysteries of the faith, enabling them to receive this love for themselves.

In this way, a new form or aid to Christian prayer was born that came to be called *meditation*. Gnostics and Hindus had practised meditation before, as well as Neoplatonists and Stoics, but that was different. In this new form of meditation, Christians could see the love of God as it was made flesh in Jesus, as it flowed out of him onto others, and was daily and continually flowing out of him and into them after the first Pentecost. From the very beginning, they were taught to pray as before at certain times of the day, most especially at nine o'clock in the morning, midday, three in the afternoon and even at midnight (the hour of Christ's birth). Now, they were taught to practise the new form of prayer that would naturally arise from their meditations. Meditation on the most loveable man who had ever existed, in the act of loving and giving himself to others, naturally led the faithful to respond to him in the language of love.

However, it eventually did even more than that. When you come to know someone closely and intimately and come to realise that they not only love you but are prepared to give their life for you, then something life-changing happens. You will want to be united with them, to be one with them at all times, to do what they do and experience all that they experience.

In ordinary circumstances, although it is possible to love someone who is dead, it is not possible to be united with them. However, we are not talking about ordinary circumstances but about the extraordinary circumstances that arose when God raised Jesus from the dead and then promised at his Ascension that he would be with those who loved him at all times, to the end of the world. This unity would be made possible through the love that drew them all up and into his Mystical Body at the first Pentecost. This new form of prayer was not make-believe or play-acting but a form of inspired meditation. It would generate the love that enabled them to enter into Christ here and now by leading them ever more deeply into his Mystical Body that would be forever with them. Christians have known and practised this form of prayer throughout subsequent centuries.

However, when meditation does generate the love enabling the Holy Spirit to lead believers into Christ's Mystical Body, a profound purification begins. This purification enables our impure and imperfect hearts to be united with Christ's pure and perfect heart as we experience the mutual loving that continually flows between him and his Father. This new development in a person's spiritual life is so important that we must describe it in far more detail because it comprises the Mystic Way as it is usually understood. If you want to make a resolution that can dramatically change your life, resolve to learn how to meditate in such a way that you can come to know and love God—present, alive, and active in the person of Jesus Christ when he was on earth.

CHAPTER 15

Holy Families

WOULD YOU WRITE ME OFF as an incurable romantic if I told you that I believe in love at first sight? I have come across it not only in fiction but in real life, too. In fact, so have you if you have read the Gospels because I believe they begin with the best example of love at first sight that I have ever come across. However, true love —I mean the true deep love that can last more than a lifetime—requires time to take root and ripen due to the many human imperfections impeding it.

When St Joseph first set eyes on the woman he was to marry, he had no imperfections hindering him from loving her instantly with his whole mind and heart. His love for her reached out to be enthralled by her physical beauty and also by her inner spiritual beauty, originating deep down within her. Like all other human beings, Joseph and Mary were created in the image and likeness of God (Genesis 1:27), but there was a difference. Mary's pure and perfect love that put no obstacles in the way of Joseph's love enabled his love to reach down within her to touch this likeness that mirrored the divine in the very depth of her being, and her love for him did likewise. The mutual loving that bonded them together and overflowed onto their Son was then inspired not only by human love but also by divine love too.

Their Son's love for them added a further supernatural dimension to their love for each other because the human love that Christ returned in kind was suffused and surcharged with the love of his heavenly Father flowing into him. In the new world order that he came to establish, Jesus wanted all families to be animated with the same love that he had infused into the family in which he grew up. That is why he poured out the same love that his Father poured out on him whilst he was on earth—onto and into all who were open to receive it, beginning at the first Pentecost.

Thanks to the promise made to Abraham in the Old Testament, family love was the only way his descendants would generate the new people who would bring salvation to the Jewish race and, ultimately, to all races. But thanks to Christ and to the love that he and his Father poured out on the first Pentecost day, the unmarried who chose to follow his own example and his call to virginity could also help generate the supernatural loving that would help build his Kingdom on earth. These people, who left all to follow the example of Christ, came to be called the *virgines et continentes*—those who chose a life of virginity from the beginning and those who chose it after their married partner had died. Although it was the family spirituality that was practised and predominated in the early Church, the virgins' spiritual influence did become ever more influential and eventually foreshadowed the later religious orders. This was especially true when they began to live not just in their own homes but in communities under the guidance of the local Bishop. The Fathers of the Church wrote special spiritual treatises to help support and inspire them. In these works, they were continually reminded that their virginity would lead to spiritual barrenness unless it was joined to the deep prayer and purification that would lead them into Mystical Contemplation and the fruits of contemplation.

For the married and the unmarried who had vowed themselves to a celibate life, the ultimate aim of their spiritual lives was to come to know and love their Risen Lord. Taken up into his Mystical Body, they mutually supported one another in being sufficiently purified for the next step in their spiritual advancement. This next step entailed being united with Christ in his loving of his Father in his Mystical Contemplation of the Three in One. Then, sharing the fruits received in this Mystical Contemplation with others, they would gradually be drawn into doing what God created us for—namely, to love, adore, and glorify him, and love others as Christ himself loved others whilst he was on earth. With the otherworldly quality of love that Christ himself came to give us, all the commandments, precepts, and moral standards that you find in the Gospels become possible because, with him and his love, all things are possible that are quite impossible without it.

Some propose that Mystical Contemplation is not for all. This is a proposition that all too many have accepted in recent years, although it has never been officially taught by the Church. Nevertheless, this extraordinary way for a few 'pious souls' would have been meaningless to our first Christian forebears. If all are called to union with God, how else could this union be realised except in, with, and through Christ? He came not just to tell us this but to show us how to be united with him in his Mystical Body and in his mystical loving of his Father. This is the essence of the God-given spirituality for which Christ lived and died. The same spirituality leads us into the fullness of life and love and the happiness for which we yearn with all our hearts. As Christ himself put it, 'I have come so that they may have life and have it to the full' (John 10:10).

We end so many of our prayers as we end the greatest of all prayers—the Eucharistic Prayer in the Mass—with the words, 'In Christ, with him, and through him, as it is only because we are one with him that our prayers, our offerings, and our sacrifices can be accepted by God. This alone enables us to share in the glory for which he originally created us. That we can participate in the sublime and divine mutual loving of the Father and the Son without the sort of prolonged mystical purification that was commonplace for all in the early Church is utter nonsense. It is the most pernicious heresy crippling contemporary spirituality.

CHAPTER 16

The Mass

ALTHOUGH CHRIST PERFORMED MOST of the religious practices that his parents taught him, there is no evidence that he offered sacrifices in the Temple. This omittance is because he came to introduce the new sacrifice 'in spirit and in truth' that he promised to the Samaritan woman. It was the sacrifice of himself. This offering of self was the sacrifice he offered to God throughout his life on earth, and which he taught his new followers to practise in their lives, too. That is why his followers were so aware of their priesthood because only they could offer themselves; no one else could do it for them. And they knew that God would accept their offering if made in the new Temple and, in, with and through the new High Priest who is Christ. This offering and acceptance is what happened sacramentally each time they went to Mass as it still is each time we go to Mass today.

When Christ was dying on the Cross, a lifetime of selfless, sacrificial loving was drawn together as one sublime action in the final, most testing and most agonising act of selfless, sacrificial loving he had ever made. At Mass, he was and still is made present to his faithful followers in performing this selfless, sacrificial action in the redemptive action that was first brought to completion on Calvary. In this way, all who are called to follow him are drawn up to share in his redeeming action for themselves and for the world that he now reaches out to through them. That is why St John quotes Christ as saying, 'And when I am lifted up from the earth, I shall draw all men to myself' (John 12:32).

At their weekly Mass, Christ was not just present as someone who had played a part in their past history but as someone who was playing a part in their present story. The mutual Divine Loving uniting him with his Father was simultaneously overflowing onto and into all those present who were open to receive him. When receiving him as the bread of life, his love would draw them up and into his Mystical Body and into his mystical loving of his Father. What came to be called the Morning Offering would enable the first faithful to offer themselves each day to God in and through their Risen Lord. In doing this day after day in their lives, as Jesus did in his life, their whole lives would gradually be transformed into the Mass. The great Jesuit liturgist Josef Andreas Jungmann put it this way: 'The Mass should so form us that the whole of our lives become the Mass, the place where we continually offer ourselves through Christ to the Father'.

This profound realisation perfectly sums up the Mystical Spirituality that inspired the early Christians and can be demonstrated by two quotations, one from St Justin and the other from St Jerome. I have mentored them before, but I mention them again because their testimony bears witness to the very essence of early Christian spirituality. St Justin was writing about a hundred years after the Crucifixion. He said that at the end of the great Eucharistic prayer, when the congregation joined with the priest at the altar in reciting the 'Amen', the sound nearly took the roof off the church where Mass was being celebrated. They knew and experienced daily that the offering made at Mass summed up the whole of their lives being offered in, with and through Christ to God. Over two hundred years later, St Jerome wrote that in his day, the sound of that same 'Amen' said by the congregation and the celebrant had not diminished; he wrote that it sounded 'like a mighty clap of thunder that resounded around the Basilica'.

This sound that resounded week after week, year after year, century after century, embodied in their full-hearted affirmation of the God-given Spirituality that Jesus Christ had first lived himself before bequeathing it to the Church he founded. That great 'Amen' was a *crie de Coeur*, pronouncing their profound faith in their Risen Lord who was not only alive and loving them continually as he had promised but was the One in whom they lived and moved and had their being. Through him, they offered themselves to the Father not just on the day they came together at Mass but on every day through all they said and did.

If this meant they would have to give their lives for their belief through bloody martyrdom, then so be it. If not, then they would willingly embrace white martyrdom instead. Regardless, the Christian way of life involved daily carrying the Cross; this enabled them to die again and again to what St Paul called the 'old man' in them so that the 'new man', full of his Father's love, would be fully formed in them. Such renewal would not only enable Christ to continue transmitting this love to others—those living in the first Christian centuries and in subsequent centuries, down to the present day.

True tradition means allowing true love to be handed on. That is what the word *tradition* means. This handing on is symbolised by the laying on of hands, through which the love of Christ continues to be transmitted to his people. For instance, the person whose hands touched you when you were baptised received Christ's loving power from the Bishop, who laid hands on him at his ordination. That *tradition*, that sacred touch, can be seamlessly traced back from Bishop to Bishop to the first Apostles and to the loving touch of Christ himself. This tradition is true in all the sacraments. We especially see it in the sacrament of marriage, when love is communicated through touch by the ministers of this sacrament of love many times each day.

Love is not magic, however. Consequently, only those who, in imitation of Christ, daily practise an ever-deepening prayer life can receive and assimilate the love given by this sacred touch. The more they pray, the more that love will enter into them and ultimately suffuse and surcharge their own weak human loving with Divine Loving. That is how true tradition is established and continues to be communicated by Christ to the world, which he wants to continue redeeming with his love through us.

CHAPTER 17

The Asceticism of the Heart

EARLY CHRISTIAN SPIRITUALITY WAS DOMINATED by a world-shaking event. Christ, whom the masses had been assured was dead, had in reality risen from the dead. He was not only alive as he had been before but glorified and animated by the love of God in an unprecedented way. Now, he would be ready and able to pour out that love like never before. This love poured out at Pentecost generated what came to be called a Mystical Body. It was Christ's new spiritual body, animated by the Holy Spirit, who would draw all who were open to receive him into itself. Before this happened, the followers of Christ would pray together with him, by his side as it were, but now they could pray in, with, and through him. The closer they were united to Christ and to his infinite loving, the more they could receive from God the love that made them more and more like him until they could say, as St Paul said, 'I live, no it is no longer I who live but Christ who lives in me' (Galatians 2:20). To keep receiving this love, we need a new form of asceticism that I will call the asceticism of the heart.

The asceticism practised by the philosophical religions that abounded in the Hellenistic world into which Christianity was born promised that if human beings could only take themselves in hand, they could make themselves perfect. Their teachers instructed them to impose a rigorous daily asceticism on themselves for self-mastery.

However, the main asceticism Jesus Christ taught his first follow-ers is that without God and without his love, we can do nothing, let alone make ourselves into paragons of virtue. There is only one form of asceticism that can make us perfect. That is what came to be called *the asceticism of the heart*. Instead of wasting time trying to do the impossible, use the same time and energy turning to the only One who can do it for you, or rather with you.

We make the same mistake with Christ as we do with the saints. We read their lives backward. We read about their rigorous lives—laden with their superhuman sacrifices and their heroic virtues—and we surmise that the only way we can be like them is to do likewise by imposing on ourselves the superhuman asceticism that we suppose galvanised them. We must instead read their lives forward instead of backward; then we would see that they were only capable of do-ing the seemingly impossible because they first received the power to do it in prayer. If we try to do what they did without first receiv-ing what they received, then our brave attempts will inevitably end in disaster. Genuine imitation of Christ or any of his saints means firstly copying the way they did all in their power to receive the same Holy Spirit who inspired and animated everything they said and did. That is essentially all we must do. That is why the spiritual life is so simple if only we have a childlike simplicity to see it.

The first Christians embraced a new form of asceticism that would not dissipate their energies trying to do the impossible but would enable them to do what Christ called 'the one thing necessary'. Above all else, this means gathering what little resources we have to create quality space and time in our daily lives for the prayer permitting us access to the same love that filled Jesus Christ and in-spired everything he said and did. Asceticism for beginners is quite simple: do not give up anything you like or enjoy except when it prevents you from giving quality space and time to God in prayer each day. If you think it is too easy, then try it and stick to it. You will soon find it is not quite as easy as you thought. Do not let first enthusiasm fool you into heroics you will never sustain. When you have persevered for long enough, you will gradually begin to receive and then experience the love that will enable you to do what is quite impossible without it.

The trouble is that the spiritual life seems to have become so complicated over the years that you almost feel you need a couple of degrees in theology just to understand it before you can even attempt to live it! Yet it is essentially simple. It is so simple that all you need is the simplicity of a little child to see it. Only one thing is necessary, and that is love. Not our love of God but his love of us. In other words, Christianity firstly teaches a Mystical Theology, not a moral theology. It is not primarily concerned with detailing the perfect moral behaviour embodied in Christ's life and then trying to copy it virtue by virtue. That is Stoicism, not Christianity, and it is doomed to failure. Christianity is primarily concerned with teaching us how to turn and open ourselves to receive the same Holy Spirit who filled Jesus Christ. The more we are filled with his love, the easier it is to return it in kind, as the divine suffuses and then surcharges human love so that it can reach up to God and out to others. Then and only then are we able to 'love God with our whole hearts and minds and with our whole beings, and to love our neighbour as Christ loves us'.

When we begin to practise the first of the new commandments in, with, and through Christ, everything else in the spiritual life falls into place. The exemplary behaviour, the extraordinary self-discipline, and the heroic sacrifices made by a person who begins to experience the love of God are not the result of an arrogant Stoic trying to perfect themselves. They are the actions of someone desperate to express their love in behaviour that could not be maintained for long without the love that sustains it. All the little pleasures and pastimes thought indispensable before suddenly become dispensable. With the greatest of ease, virtues that were noticeable by their absence before are born of the love that envelops them. In short, first seek God and his Kingdom of love, and all else will be given to you.

CHAPTER 18

A Whistle-Stop History of Catholic Spirituality

1. The Resuscitation of Pelagianism

WINSTON CHURCHILL SAID THAT THOSE WHO FAIL to learn from history are condemned to repeat it. That is why I want to offer you a brief history of Catholic Spirituality so that what pertains to its very essence can be seen. It will show how history has distorted it and how we can return to it as it was introduced into the early Church by Christ himself. All the other religions that thrived in the Greco-Roman world into which Christianity was born did not primarily seek God's love to transform them but rather their own human endeavour. This set of beliefs infiltrated Christianity and was championed by the British Monk Pelagius. Thanks to great saints like St Augustine, these Pelagian heresies which overemphasised the action of the human spirit at the expense of the Holy Spirit, were kept at bay.

Due to a handful of heretics, the simple Christ-centred spirituality prevailing in the early Church was obfuscated in the Dark Ages. With the reopening of the Holy Land to pilgrims in the wake of the Crusaders, Christ-centred spirituality returned in the twelfth century. It spread throughout Christendom with the help of great saints such as St Bernard of Clairvaux and St Francis of Assisi. This spirituality, which was lived and practised most particularly in the family, was sustained and strengthened in subsequent centuries by new religious practices like the Rosary, the Stations of the Cross, and devotion to the Sacred Heart which helped the faithful return to the essence of early Christian spirituality. Who is the Sacred Heart but the Risen Christ, love Incarnate continually pouring out his love on all who would receive it?

However, after the Great Plague (1348-1350), many began to ask how such a loving God could allow half of Europe to die in such a terrible way, and they began looking elsewhere for religious inspiration. At this very point in history (circa 1350), the rise of the Renaissance enabled those who questioned their faith to rediscover various philosophical religions, such as Stoicism, Gnosticism, and Neoplatonism, which the early Church had deemed heretical. A new brand of Catholic intelligentsia came to champion a high-bred form of spirituality owing as much to Socrates of Athens as to Jesus of Nazareth.

This new high-bred form of Catholicism found its way into the contemporary education system, thanks to Catholic humanists such as John Colet. John Colet was a wealthy Catholic priest, the son of the lord mayor of London and a friend of Erasmus. Colet founded St Paul's school in 1509, the year Henry VIII was crowned King. In this school, all the intellectual glories of the Renaissance were embodied in an academic education system followed by all other schools and institutes of further education down to the present day.

Ever since, students like me have been confused, as the simple God-centred spirituality learnt at home was contradicted by a complex make-yourself-perfect spirituality owing as much to the Stoic philosopher Marcus Aurelius as to Jesus Christ. The Pelagian Stoicism of Marcus Aurelius taught how we should turn to ourselves to make ourselves perfect. On the other hand, the God-given spirituality of Jesus Christ taught us how to turn to God to enable him to make us perfect through his Holy Spirit, the only true architect of holiness.

From this point onward, two spiritual trends paralleled each other in Catholic theology and spirituality. The new trend that was born at what has come to be called the birth of the modern world—the Renaissance—emphasised human endeavour and was man-centred or anthropocentric in a way completely at odds with early Christian theocentric spirituality.

Humanism's Credo is 'I believe in Man', whilst Christianity's Credo is 'I believe in God'. With the rise of the Enlightenment and Quietism (a Protestant form of mysticism) at the end of the seventeenth century, the Mystical Theology and spirituality that had prevailed since the early Church came under attack. The Mystical Theology that taught union with Christ and depended on a profound inner purification in prayer was not only ridiculed but vehemently opposed, both outside but inside the Church. Consequently, the anthropocentric spiritualities growing out of the Renaissance began prevailing above all others down to the present day. The new liturgy introduced at the Vatican Council reproduced the ancient liturgy of the early Church. Unfortunately, it did not also reintroduce the God-given spirituality that sustained and supported it.

As I grew up breathing in this spiritual ethos in a classical education system born out of the Renaissance, I thought the sanctity to which I aspired would be primarily the result of my own efforts. I was, in effect, a Christian Stoic, a Pelagian who had failed so comprehensively to make myself into the saint of my dreams that I was about to give up the spiritual life for good. Fortunately, I came across *Pax Animae*, written by a Spanish Franciscan in 1588. This spiritual gem was untouched by the spirit of Humanism. Reading it was the nearest I came to a Damascus Road experience. It immediately enabled me to see that I had been misled into believing I could be the architect of my own perfection. The very first paragraph showed me why I had failed and what I ought to do to succeed. It read thus:

With love you may bring your heart to do whatsoever you may please. The hardest things become easy and pleasant, but without love you will find anything not only difficult but also impossible.

I am grateful to this little book because it enabled me to return to the simple spirituality that prevailed in the early Church, which, due to a handful of heretics, had been muddied and muddled in the Dark Ages and then turned into a confusing high-bred spirituality at the Renaissance that still confuses the faithful to this day. Following in the footsteps of St John Henry Newman, I am trying to lead you back to the God-given Spirituality introduced into the early Church by Our Lord Jesus Christ, in which his love reigns supreme.

CHAPTER 19

A Whistle Stop History of Catholic Spirituality

2. The Curse of Quietism

EVEN THE MOST CONSERVATIVE and partisan Catholics cannot help but be disgusted by the sexual depravity and greed of the Renaissance Popes. Beyond question, their depravity influenced Martin Luther to break away from the Church in 1517 to begin the Protestant Reformation. However, this regrettable behaviour was not mirrored at ground level.

This dissonance can be verified by any objective scholar who has read about the massive spiritual reforms that changed religious orders in Europe during the fifteenth century. This profound faith could be seen most especially in England in the following centuries when a new Age of Martyrs witnessed the strength of the faith of our own Recusant ancestors. They can be studied in the works of great Catholic historians like Monsignor Philip Hughes. That these reforms reached out to influence the ordinary faithful can be read in Professor Eamon Duffy's book, *Stripping of the Altars,* which once and for all has given the lie to the reformer's contention that the ordinary Catholic laity were festering in a world of religious superstition and immorality.

When the Council of Trent was called, it was not because of the state of the Catholic faith at ground level, where my own ancestors were being imprisoned, tortured, and put to death for the faith they refused to give up. I am myself a direct descendent of Sir Nicholas Tempest, who was hanged, drawn and quartered at Tyburn in 1537 for standing up for his faith against Henry VIII, who had lost his. The Mass for which my ancestors suffered and died in penal times was represented in a new and glorious liturgy at the Council of Trent. In future, this Mass— Christ's own mystical sacrifice—was made present in such a way that the faithful felt drawn to participate in it and in Christ's own mystical worship of his Father.

This Mass stood at the centre of a Mystical Spirituality that, according to such great spiritual historians as Bremond, Tanqueray, Cognet, Pourrat, Garrigou LaGrange OP, Poulain SJ, and others, reached its heights in the hundred years after the Council of Trent. In his life's work, *Enthusiasm,* Monsignor Ronald Knox puts it this way:

The seventeenth century was a century of mystics. The doctrine of the interior life was publicized, developed in far greater detail than it had ever been in late-medieval Germany or late-medieval England. Bremond, in his *Histoire littéraire du sentiment religieux en France*, has traced unforgettably the progress of that movement in France. But Spain too, the country of St Teresa and St John of the Cross, had her mystics. Italy too had her mystics who flourished under the aegis of the Vatican. Even the exiled Church in England produced in Father Baker's *Sancta Sophia* a classic of the interior life. (Chapter XI)

To the general reader, it would seem inexplicable that this spirituality should suddenly cease because of a heresy called Quietism, condemned in 1687. But this heresy contained within it what were considered at the time to be the worst possible abominations that had to be obliterated at all costs—namely, a conversion to Protestantism and serious indulgence in gross sexual sins, as detailed by Monsignor Ronald Knox in his book *Enthusiasm* chapters XI–XII. The first Protestants believed human beings were intrinsically evil; thus, any idea of union with Christ let alone with God, was out of the question. Consequently, Mystical Prayer to that end was a non-starter. If they did seek to experience God in prayer, they could do no more than wait on him in total inactivity, as no human action, let alone merit, could induce God to act. So, when the founder of Quietism, the Spanish Priest Molinos, taught his followers to do nothing in Mystical Prayer nor to do anything if sexual temptations should afflict them, he was condemned as charged. That charge for which he was found guilty and given a life sentence was of leading his followers into Protestantism and into serious sexual sins.

The outrage in the Church at the time cannot be underestimated. For the first time in the Church, Mystical Prayer wrongly came to be seen as not only dangerous but a practice that had to be suppressed everywhere. The subsequent anti-mystical witch hunts threw out the baby with the bath water, as any form of spirituality that had the slightest whiff of Quietism about it had to be rooted out. Their endeavours were so successful that down to the present day, Mystical Theology has been undermined, if not positively condemned, and what the Church historian Louis Cognet called 'Christian Humanism' has taken over.

In his monumental *History of the Church,* Monsignor Philip Hughes wrote:

The most mischievous feature of Quietism was the suspicion that it threw on the contemplative life as a whole. At the moment when, more than at any other, the Church needed the strength that only the life of contemplation can give, it was the tragedy of history that this life shrank to very small proportions, and religion, even for holy souls, too often took on the appearance of being no more than a divinely aided effort towards moral perfection.

This moral perfection included the moral teaching of the Gospels and also the moral teaching of Stoicism that had seeped into Christianity in the third and fourth centuries and, again, as we have seen at the Renaissance. Upon the permanent undermining of the Mystical Theology that had for over seventeen hundred years taught believers how to die to self in order to live in, with and through Christ, something else took its place. A plethora of private devotions and popular piety produced a pick-and-mix spirituality to which I have already referred. It expanded to assume its place in striking contrast to the simplicity of the God-given Spirituality of love that Christ introduced into the early Church. Undeniably, many, if not most, of these devotional practices are good and have been found helpful for all too many sheep without shepherds. Nevertheless, we must return to the Spirituality God gave us and learn from our earliest forebears. This spirituality is so clear, simple, and totally transforming, for it transforms us into being one with Christ in our prayer life, in our daily life, and in our liturgical life. That is why I must now continue to describe and detail it for all, because it is for all who know how to receive God's love, and how to return it in kind.

CHAPTER 20

A Whistle-Stop History of Catholic Spirituality

3. From Trent to Vatican II

FOR MOST PEOPLE TODAY, the greatest glory of the Council of Trent was the Tridentine Mass with which I grew up. For one hundred years or more after the Council, it perfectly embodied the mystical action of Christ and also the Mystical Spirituality that was open to the faithful. It was this that enabled them to be so purified in their Mystical Prayer life that they could be more perfectly united with Christ in his Mystical Prayer made present in the Sacrifice of the Mass.

The selfless, sacrificial giving that is first practised in Mystical Prayer beyond first emotional beginnings gradually creates a general habit of selfless, sacrificial giving. It is this that step by step enables our whole lives outside of prayer to resemble the selfless, sacrificial life that Christ lived while he was on earth. Then, we can be more perfectly united with him when we go to Mass each Sunday with our spiritual brothers and sisters. This selfless, sacrificial giving is nothing other than the true love that, with genuine human endeavour suffused with divine love, grows out of the juvenile love written about by poets and sung about by pop stars. However, it takes years rather than months to establish itself in those who seek it and then flourishes only with the love that pours out of the Risen Christ.

What was lost to a handful of heretics in the early Church was lost again due to Molinos and his heresy of Quietism in 1687. When the mature adult loving learnt in Mystical Prayer was all but condemned, the faithful had to turn to a far more superficial pick-and-mix spirituality. Many have wrongly surmised that this inherently fragmented spirituality has come down to us from the Council of Trent in harness with the Tridentine Mass and that the two are, therefore, different sides of the same coin, which they are certainly not. It was not just that this splintered spirituality is in itself so diffuse and disconnected, but that its different orientations do not naturally lead to what should be their natural and preordained consummation in the Mass. In short, they obfuscated the true God-given spirituality given to the early Church by Christ himself and its superb and sublime conclusion in the Mass.

In the same way that the Great Plague coincided with the beginning of the rise of the Renaissance in the middle of the thirteenth century, the condemnation of Quietism coincided with the rise of the Enlightenment at the end of the seventeenth century. This occurrence further damaged the reputation of Mystical Prayer, causing its demise as the new age condemned everything that could not be subjected to the analysis of pure reason. Inevitably, Mystical Theology was considered not only spiritually dangerous but irrational. Truly, it is supra-rational because its formal object is the purification of our love by divine love in such a way that we can be united with God.

The Enlightenment influenced all European institutions, including the Church. If renewal could no longer come from God's love and those mystics and saints who have been purified to receive it, then it must come from man's reason and those who taught how to use it. Henceforth, the Thomistic Theology that the Church used to express herself at the Council of Trent was used to renew the Church. I studied this theology during the last Thomist revival at the end of the nineteen-fifties. It seems that those who have championed these intellectual renewals have conveniently forgotten that St Thomas never finished his great work because after experiencing the love of God in what St Teresa of Avila later called the Mystical Marriage, he changed dramatically. He deemed all that he had written thus far as mere straw and then laid down his pen. The great *Summa Theologica* was never finished!

The dry intellectualism of my scholastic theological studies was suddenly revived by what came to be called the 'New Biblical Theology'. The Christian Enlightenment encouraged new, deeper, and more critical biblical scholarship that illuminated how the Old Testament was brought to perfection in the New Testament and on the lives and liturgical practices of the first faithful. However, although this new theology was extremely exciting and helpful, it did not go deep enough. All the scholars had been brought up without the profound Mystical Theology extracted from religious education. This meant they were denied the first gift of contemplative loving which is the infused virtue of wisdom contained in that loving. This omission prevented them from seeing and understanding in any depth the profound mystical teaching that Christ had bequeathed to the first Christians.

When Jean Daniélou SJ produced his dazzling masterwork, *Bible and the Liturgy*, a contemporary reviewer described it as 'brilliant but superficial'. Such criticism could be said of all the great scholars whose scholarship had such an influence on The Second Vatican Council and, for that matter, of me and many others! Although this scholarship helped to produce what, to most of the laity, was a new liturgy in their own language that, in many ways, replicated the ancient Christian liturgy, it did not go far enough. Because their scholarship was not deep enough, they failed to produce a comparable document detailing the deep mystical dimensions of the early Christian spirituality expressed in the Mass.

The pick-and-mix spiritualities that have proliferated down to the present day can so easily cause disagreement, disharmony, and discordance in contrast to the simple God-given spirituality that determined the daily lives of the first Christians. This spirituality that Christ himself introduced that made them one in him, in everything they said and did. It was this spirituality of true love that expressed itself in the same sort of selfless, sacrificial giving that Christ first lived himself, which found its fullest communal expression in their weekly Mass. There, they received according to the measure they gave; and what they received was the only love that, through them, could and did change the world in which they were living.

CHAPTER 21

A Whistle-Stop History of Catholic Spirituality

4. A God-centred Spirituality

CHRISTIAN SPIRITUALITY WAS FIRST LIVED by Jesus Christ himself before it was introduced into the early Church. It began with him practising the First Commandment—love God with every fibre of his being in all that he said and did. He was then open to receive God's love in return at every moment of his life. That is why Christ taught his followers to follow him in doing this so that they would receive from God the same love that made him the most loveable, the most perfect, and the most adorable person who has ever lived.

In the scriptures, God's love is repeatedly symbolised by and likened to light. As Sir Isaac Newton has shown, a single shaft of light contains within itself all the colours that enable creation to reflect God's glory on earth in such an awe-inspiring way. Just as these colours can be seen when light strikes a prism, so all the infused gifts of God's love can be seen when that love strikes a human heart—to be diffused into every part of the human personality. Gradually, if a person perseveres in the Mystical Prayer that purifies them ever more fully to receive this love, then something dramatic happens. Just as it did in Christ himself, it can be seen suffusing and transforming everything they say and do. That is why St Teresa of Avila said, 'There is only one way to perfection and that is to pray. If anyone points in another direction, then they are deceiving you'.

These 'deceivers' are not consciously trying to deceive you or anyone else for that matter. They have the best will in the world, but they themselves have been misled by others who have been caught up in a pernicious historical tidal wave contaminated with Pelagianism. This deceit has led them to believe that they can become the architects of their own perfection, with a nominal nod to the grace of God if questioned about their orthodoxy. Authentic Catholic spirituality is totally different; indeed, it is the very opposite. It means, above all else, seeking quality daily space and time each day to come to know and love God in prayer, knowing that his love alone will do what nobody else and nothing else can. However, post-Renaissance Catholic asceticism has primarily come to mean changing oneself through man-made forms of Stoical asceticism.

Since the Second Vatican Council, a new variant of this asceticism has spread. Instead of seeking perfection through man-made forms of asceticism inspired by Stoicism, it has now become the practice to pursue it through pop psychology in one guise or another. Most human beings need some form of psychological help in their lifetime, and they must be encouraged to seek it to enable them to return to their normal selves. However, pop psychology (or any form of psychology) cannot transform a person through love into the most perfect person who can alone guide us to and unite us with God. In the wrong hands, terrible harm can and has been done to others, including to whole communities, by believing and behaving as if socio-psychological techniques can achieve what only God's love can do in Mystical Prayer.

Many years ago, I knew a man who was a Benedictine oblate because he had a penchant for Gregorian chant and the monastic life. Whilst wearing a Carmelite scapular because he felt drawn to Mystical Prayer, he practised Jesuit spirituality, which does not officially practise or promote Mystical Prayer. However, his wise selection from the current pick-and-mix spiritualities saved him from a non-mystical muddle. The picture of the Sacred Heart that hung in his home continually reminded him of God's love. The quality of this love was brought home to him whenever he made the Stations of the Cross. Each time he said the Rosary, his faith was deepened as he learned to penetrate the great mysteries of our faith. When these devotional practices set alight what St Augustine called a yearning for union with God, he turned to a spiritual director to teach him the meditation that leads to that union through Mystical Contemplation. It was then that he was inspired, like St John Henry Newman, to study the ancient sources of Catholic Spirituality in all its simplicity.

T.S. Eliot once said, 'The end of all our exploring will be to arrive where we started and to know that place for the first time'. In discovering the spirituality Christ first lived himself, the Benedictine oblate found that, although it was embodied in the devotions parents had taught him, the way it was originally practised re-inspired his dedication to serious daily Mystical Prayer. This prayer became the most crucial feature of his daily spirituality. Furthermore, he found that, in moments of darkness, he could still return to some of the devotional practices, like the Rosary, that had originally formed him, albeit in a new way that helped support him in the Mystic Way. With the Love of God that he was learning in selfless, sacrificial loving central to his daily prayer, he was able to receive the pure love of God that contains within it all the infused virtues and gifts. With these profound gifts of the Holy Spirit, he found that, for the first time, he was able to observe the second of the New Commandments that Christ gave us shortly before he died—not just to love others as we love ourselves, but much more. We must love others as Christ himself loves us.

True Catholic Mystical Prayer is God-centred. It is not the pursuit of self-gratifying psychological states or esoteric experiences through man-made techniques to attain instant 'mysticism'. These counterfeit forms of 'Mystical Prayer' are more like self-interested cupboard-loving than unconditional mother-loving. They are usually referred to as *mysticism*, a word that the Church Fathers never used. Only the same sort of selfless, sacrificial loving that characterised the life of Christ should characterise the prayer of those who follow him. This quality of loving learnt in Mystical Prayer opens a believer to God's love and enables that love to possess them. Without the selflessness that is learnt there, we will continually remain closed to the Only One whose Love makes all things new.

CHAPTER 22

A Whistle-Stop History of Catholic Spirituality

5. Back to the Future

BEFORE I FINISH MY WHISTLE-STOP TOUR of Catholic spirituality, I want to draw your attention to an interesting shift in the authority of the Catholic Church after Quietism that has had unfortunate consequences for contemporary Catholics. Firstly, with the demise of contemplative prayer, there was a corresponding demise of the fruits of contemplative prayer, including wisdom. This demise put the Church at an intellectual disadvantage when combating the rise of so many new and dangerous ideas during the rise of the Enlightenment in Europe. Therefore, both her intellectual and spiritual authority were, therefore, undermined since the demise of contemplative prayer. When the French Revolution seemed to further take away the Church's physical authority, at least in France and threatened to do likewise in other countries, the Vatican felt that it was seriously losing its authority.

However, as time passed, the Church gradually began to realise that free of interfering monarchs like the King of France, she was able to have far greater personal authority than before. Through the hierarchy, whom it could now appoint with far greater freedom than ever before, she suddenly found that she could have far greater authority than previously. This authority was further emphasised by the proclamation of Papal Infallibility at the First Vatican Council in the nineteenth century. Losing the Papal states to the newly formed Italian state might have diminished this newfound authority, but what might have been lost in the form of physical presence in Italy was actually gained in worldwide presence through her own centrally appointed hierarchy.

This spiritual presence was now supported by using the administration once created to govern the papal states to build up a worldwide system of administration. It also created an international intelligence network that, in recent years, has been described as second to none worldwide. What has been called 'galloping infallibility' has enabled modern Popes to amass far greater power for the papacy than at any other time in the Church's history. As long as this power was used in service, as Christ himself insisted, then all would have been well. However, power has an unfortunate tendency to proliferate in the hands of powerful potentates; furthermore, they are reluctant to ever give it away on any pretext. That this power has been used for good is beyond question, just as it is beyond question that it has recently been used for evil.

Over sixty years ago, this power overreached itself in 1960 when, according to Cardinal Bea, papal power decided to keep what was called the third secret of Fatima hidden from the faithful. This fateful misuse of authority was destined to have terrible consequences. It was a decision ratified by several Popes, some of whom were canonised. Canonisation does not mean that a person is free from sin and pride that is the besetting sin of powerful magnates who were responsible for refusing to listen to Our Lady's call to repentance at Fatima and at many other appearances before and since. If only they had, like the little children to whom Our Lady appeared, truly believed in her message and acted upon the warnings therein! Then, the terrible consequences that we have already experienced, with much more mayhem to come, could have been avoided. Undoubtedly, Pelagianism, the besetting sin of the proud, persuaded the Pope to call a Council to do for the Church through man-made wisdom which only Our Lady's call to repentance could do. If instead of calling 'the Council of Ambiguity', the Pope and his successors had called for a worldwide crusade of personal prayer and repentance, our present plight would have long since been evaded. The tragedy is that sixty or more years ago, the Church did not just listen to Our Lady and then harnessed, organised, and led the faithful to radically renew their lives. If she had, then the crusade to end all crusades may by now have been well and done, and what had been lost since Quietism would now be back in place. Sadly, due to a lack of leadership and guidance, over a hundred years or more of Marian pilgrimages seems to have borne little deep and lasting fruit.

It has been calculated that there have been many thousands, if not millions more Catholics, who have visited Marian shrines in the last hundred and fifty or more years than there were Catholics in the early Christian centuries. Notice that it is essentially the same spirituality, but there is a dramatic difference. While the first Christians transformed an ancient pagan world into a Christian world in such a short time, Marian pilgrims have had little if any comparable impact on the contemporary Church, never mind the world. The difference is quite clear. The first Christians radically practised the faith that had been given to them. Meanwhile, modern Marian pilgrims have spent so much time revelling in miracles, prophecies, esoteric phenomena, and revelations that they have forgotten to practise, and practise daily, what Our Lady came to teach them. It is one thing to be inspired; it is quite another thing to put into practice what Our Lady wants us to do. The trouble is, believers still think they can have and enjoy all the full panoply of pleasure offered to them by the modern world while simultaneously growing in the spiritual life by practising daily and deeply what Our Lady called upon us to practise in her more recent appearances: repentance, and time for prayer.

The key word is *Time*. If you want to achieve any manner of success in any form of human achievement, it means giving time to learning. We must learn to play the piano, speak a foreign language, play some form of sport, earn a degree at university, and master and maintain one's knowledge of one of the professions. If a person only gives the same time to contemplation as to mastering and maintaining one's proficiency on the piano, for instance, then contemplation would soon become for modern Catholics what it was in the early Church and what it was in the Tridentine Spirituality before the curse of Quietism.

However, as we have all witnessed, although this radical crusade was not to be, the Church nevertheless continues to press on, regardless, with its totalitarian system of spiritual power still perfectly intact. The terrible irony is that this power that Our Lady wanted to be harnessed for good has been harnessed for evil instead. With generations of Catholics used to giving blind obedience to papal authority like never before in her history, it was a comparatively simple matter to introduce radical and dramatic changes without most of the faithful noticing it. Pseudo-orthodoxy has been introduced instead of orthodoxy, false tradition instead of true tradition, while gradually destroying every monastery or convent that practised the contemplative life. prayer and contemplation harness the Holy Spirit, who is their greatest threat.

What had generally been a benign autocracy suddenly changed into a vicious and vindictive dictatorship for all who would not subscribe to the dismantling of their Church and the building up of a false Church, founded not on divine but on human wisdom. Sacrifice was out; self-service, self-satisfaction, and self-indulgence were in. Lust would replace love, and every restriction would be replaced by licence. Every priest, every Bishop, every Cardinal who stood out against this modern iconoclasm would be cancelled in one way or another, ensuring the silence of the others and leaving the sheep at the mercy of the wolves. Such strategy is a classic tactic of the Marxism that is their blueprint for the anti-Catholic revolution.

There is only one way forward from where we are now, and that is backward into the future. We must return to the God-given spirituality that Jesus Christ Our Lord first lived before introducing it to the early Church. That is, of course, the ongoing subject of this book.

CHAPTER 23

The Hypostatic Union

WHEN ST AUGUSTINE SAID that our hearts are restless until they rest in God, he was speaking not just of other Christians but of all human beings. He meant all human beings because we are all made in the image and likeness of God (Genesis 1:26). The question is how we get from here—from where we are now—to the God who has created us to share in his own inner life and eternal loving for which we crave. It was to answer this question that Christ came.

That is why he said that he is The Way, The Truth, and The Life. He is 'The Way' because it would only be in, with, and through him that our hearts that yearn for God would find him. He is 'The Truth' because the ultimate truth that God is Love was literally embodied in his human physical body. Because this truth was re-alised in his human being, he could tell other human beings this sublime truth while simultaneously explaining that, through him, they would be able to experience something of this infinite love as he did, even beginning in this life. He is also 'The Life' because the fullness of life, which is love, the fullness of love for which we yearn, can only be found in him because he is in God and God is in him (John 14:6-10). When we try to observe the Commandments, as Jesus promised at the Last Supper, then he can make his home in us, and we can make our home in him so that all our deepest desires and hopes and yearnings are fulfilled (John 14:21-24). This union enables us to experience true, if interrupted, happiness in this life and true, uninterrupted happiness in the next.

St Paul called God's stupendous plan to share his infinite life and loving with us the *Mysterion*. This Greek word means *unseen, invisible or secret* because the plan is visible only to the eye of faith. This word is the origin of the word *mystic*, used in the Catholic tradition to describe a person who is totally committed to entering into God's Plan, the *Mysterion*. In the Old Testament, the prophets did not detail this plan because they did not know it in detail themselves, but they did promise those who were waiting that it would be explained in more detail when Christ came. Even after telling his followers what it would involve for them and those who would follow them, Christ said that it had not come yet. However, he promised that God's plan for them that had already come in him would, in only a short time, come for them when the final preparations were in place—preparations that only he could bring about.

These preparations were in place after his Ascension when his physical human body was united with his Father in such a way that it was glorified by being possessed as never before by the infinite loving that had reigned in God from eternity. The preparations were now in place because his physical human body that had restricted him to being in only one place at a time while he was on earth and present therefore only to those in that place was radically changed by the infinite loving that now possessed him. His whole human and divine personality suddenly expanded spiritually in such a way that it could be present to people in every place on earth and in every subsequent century.

His new transformed and transfigured body came to be called his mystical body, not just because it could be present to every human being on earth simultaneously, but because his body became porous so that the love that was animating him from the inside would overflow onto and into all who were open to receive it, as happened on the first Pentecost day. On the first Pentecost, this loving was symbolised by fire, but on subsequent occasions, when his love was poured out onto and into individuals at their Baptism, it was symbolised by water.

Both fire and water then symbolised the inner divine spirit that animated Christ in a unique way after he was fully transformed and transfigured when he was glorified after his Ascension into heaven. This same divine Spirit first possessed Christ before it was communicated to us. As a mark of reverence, this divine spirit has been called The Holy Spirit. This Holy Spirit that first animated Christ is transmitted to us so that it can become the sacred ligature that binds us together with him, in his mystical body, and with all others in that body so that we can support one another as we travel together in The Way, and on the way, from here to eternity.

Let me try to explain what is and will forever remain a profound mystery by turning to a human metaphor in the form of a story that happened to me some years ago to explain what has come to be called the Hypostatic Union.

It was a disaster waiting to happen, and it did happen when I absentmindedly plugged my 12-volt kettle into the mains. I can still see the sparks flying, the smoke rising, and the smell of rubber burning as the kettle I had bought for the car languished and died before me. At least I learnt a valuable lesson. Two hundred and forty limitless volts of electricity will not go into a 12-volt receiver. Nor, therefore, would God's limitless love go into a limited human receiver, at least not without a transformer. That is why God sent Christ to become a living, breathing spiritual transformer because he had both a divine and a human nature. This meant that he could plug in, as it were, to God's infinite love in such a way that it could percolate through into his human nature. In this way, the same love that animated him could be transmitted to all other human natures—all other men and women—who were open to receive it and to the end of time. That is why he became, and still is for us now, The Way, The Truth, and the Life.

CHAPTER 24

The One Thing Necessary

WHEN THE CHURCH WAS BORN on the first Pentecost day, it was as poor as Christ when he was born on the first Christmas day. It had nothing but love. But that love was more than enough because it was the love of God, his Holy Spirit, which poured out upon it and into it, from the Risen and recently Glorified body of Christ. When this Good News was proclaimed by St Peter and his Apostles, who had just received it the crowds begged them to explain how they could receive this love too, for they had already seen for themselves what it did for these men whose mystical transformation they had at first mistaken for drunkenness.

The terrible and savage cruelty of Christ's horrific death on the Cross had determined that there were no more than a hundred and twenty followers who dared to come to witness his Ascension into heaven. However, after Pentecost, there were three thousand who, like the Apostles themselves, were baptised into the new Church, a new religion that grew out of the old religion to which they belonged. All who received this new baptism were drawn up into the new Mystical Body of Christ like an irresistible magnetic force. When they awoke the following day, the new religion to which they had committed themselves was still poor. It had no physical structure, nor for that matter did it have any spiritual structure. It had no Creed, no systematic theology, no catechism, no apologetics, no liturgy, and no worked-out moral theology. It had only a very simple, rudimentary Mystical Theology. They had been reborn into the Mystical Body of the long-awaited Messiah who had come to take them home. Thus, they called their new religion 'The Way', after the One whom they now came to know and love as The Way, The Truth, and The Life.

With no physical or spiritual structure on which to depend, they continued to avail themselves of the old religion as before. They still performed the old religious practices and prayers as before in their own homes, in the synagogues, and in the Temple, where they tried to nurture the newfound mystical faith within their Messiah. He had returned, as promised, to be with them to the end of time. He was continually pouring out onto them the mystical love that would gradually bind them to himself and then unite them with their common Father, not just in his Mystical Body but in, with, and through his mystical loving of their now common Father. They might have nothing else, but they did have the 'one thing necessary' from which all else would grow as from a simple single mustard seed.

The love they received in return was not just a single gift from God, but it contained all the other gifts that are always the sign of authentic love. They wanted to know the truth, the whole truth, and then do the truth. They wanted justice and peace, and all that was necessary to maintain it. They wanted freedom for the oppressed, food for the starving, clothes for the naked, and equality for the downtrodden. They wanted to cast off more than six hundred rules and regulations that their old religion had insisted were necessary to please God. Soon, not only were doors closed once these new 'heretics' were seen in their true colours, but they were cruelly persecuted by their one-time co-religionists, like Saul of Tarsus. Modern scripture scholars and biblical theologians have rightly excited their students, like me, by showing how the Old Testament found its fulfilment in the New Testament. However, it is not in seeing how the old finds its fulfilment in the new but in seeing how the new infinitely transcends the old that the true mystical dimensions of early Christian spirituality can be rediscovered. These unforeseen mysteries were too much for their erstwhile spiritual brothers and sisters to comprehend.

They still shared the same God and they both believed that he loved them, but Jesus had taught them much more. The God—whom they were taught dwelt in light inaccessible, who was so holy and so distant that they could not even write down, never mind utter his name—was not only with them but in them. The God, with whom contact would mean instant death, had made his home within them. The God who had been called Father only because he created them was now to be called Dad (Abba) because he had lovingly breathed into them his own breath of life so that they could be with him and in him to eternity, sharing in the life and love of the Three in One. For the God in whom their forebears believed did not just love them, but he was, or rather is, Love. Just as in all love, there are two; so also, there are two persons in God. However, the love that unites them together is a person in his own right because he both gives and receives the love that bonds them all together. This person is called the Holy Spirit. So, the old Jews were horrified to be told that God is not just One but three in One; furthermore, their promised Messiah was, in fact, the second person of this mystical vortex of life and loving, which is God—their God, Yahweh.

Furthermore, he had come to take those who were open to receive him into the life and infinite loving of the Three in One to experience the glory that infinite mutual loving had made of them. Gradually, as they were cast off and had to construct their own religion, all these differences would inspire every facet of the newfound faith, from the Creed that summed up that faith to every detail of their daily prayer that found its natural completion and consummation in the weekly liturgy. On the first morning, however, they knew only one thing; fortunately, it was the 'one thing necessary'. That 'one thing necessary' was that Jesus had entered into them through love. The more they kept turning and opening themselves to receive that love through repentance, then, as St Peter told them, they would be taken up into him and into his loving of his Father, beginning now and ending in eternity.

They had to do only one thing and keep doing that one thing—the one thing necessary. That was to practise, and practise continually, what I have called the 'asceticism of the heart'. This practised prayer opens our hearts to the heart of God, through the heart and through the mystical loving of Christ for his Father.

CHAPTER 25

The Living Temple

ONE OF THE MOST SURPRISING TRUTHS I learnt when I first started to study scripture was that there is no record of Christ going into the Temple to offer sacrifice. The reason was because he had come to set up a new Temple just as he promised the Samaritan woman (John 4:21-25). It was a Temple that would not be made by human hands but by the hand of God on the first Easter Day. Jesus himself had foretold its coming in his own person. 'Destroy this Temple', he said, referring to his own physical body, 'and in three days I will raise it up again' (John 2:19). This New Temple would come to be called Christ's Mystical Temple or his Mystical Body because, unlike his physical body, it could not be seen. But every new Christian knew that just as on the first Easter Night, when this New Temple was raised up, they too would be raised up. This resurrection would take place on their own personal Easter Night when, after rising from the baptismal pool, they would rise to enter into Christ, the new Temple, to worship God.

In the old Temple, this worship would be embodied in some form of physical offering, such as sheep, lambs or oxen. However, in the new offering, worship would be embodied in a spiritual offering, which was nothing other than the offering of themselves. This offering was the same that Christ himself had made throughout his life on earth, and that is why he never offered any physical sacrifice in the old Temple and why he promised this new form of worship to the Samaritan woman. In other words, they were to offer a sacrifice, in spirit and in truth, that was nothing other than themselves.

Because they were offering themselves at their baptism, the first Christians were clothed in a white garment, similar to the one Christ wore at his Resurrection; this pure garment showed how they were now one with him in his new life and his new offering. They were led in procession to participate in the Mass and to exercise their priesthood by offering the new worship in spirit and in truth—namely, the offering of themselves in, with, and through Christ. They would then see and experience that they were not just one with Christ's human being, now the New Temple, but with his human action, suffused and surcharged with the divine, as the new High Priest, in, with, and through whom they would offer themselves to God the Father. Christ's sublime mystical loving was like a supernatural superhighway over which the sacrifice of himself rose to God his Father, simultaneously enabling his Father's love to descend into him. That is why Christ now became 'The Way', the spiritual superhighway, not just for his own journey back to his Father, but for those others too, who were reborn into his Mystical Body and into his mystical loving of his Father. In this way, their sacrifices would be joined with his and rise with his to receive in return the same love that he himself had received.

The bread and wine used at Mass were not just a symbol or a sacrament of Christ's whole life and afterlife; they were also the real flesh and blood embodiment of himself and his supreme sacrificial action. This substantial embodiment enabled all who received this sacred food and drink to enter into Christ, in the act of offering himself to the Father, in an act of pure Mystical Contemplation and, therefore, to receive the mystical fruits of contemplation in return. These fruits may well be mystical in themselves, but when they began to possess the receiver, they would be made visible in the infused virtues and in the fruits and gifts of the Holy Spirit that would enable them to love others as Christ had loved them.

Because Jesus was born like his mother without sin, nothing in him prevented his Father's love from continually pouring into him and remaining with him at all times during his life on earth and during his life in heaven. However, because we were not immaculately conceived, our propensity to fall into selfishness and sin means that we cannot experience the love of God as he did at all times. Consequently, we need the same Holy Spirit who drew us up into Christ's risen glory to purify and prepare us for the permanent union with God to which we are called. The more we are purified, the more deeply we can enter into the New Temple—our Risen Lord—to be united with him. The closer this union and the more deeply we are united with him, the more potent and more powerful our prayer becomes, not just when we offer ourselves to God every time we come to Mass, but the more deeply we enter into him. By entering into him, I do not just mean at Holy Communion during the Mass but after we have returned to the weekdays that make up most of our lives after weekly Mass. Every morning when we wake up, we should remember what is true whether we feel it or not—that we are within the New Temple, which is Christ.

Thus, the moment we realise where we are and whom we are within, we offer the forthcoming day to God through the New High Priest. He will always be close to us as we try to keep turning and offering ourselves to God directly whenever we pray in the forthcoming day. We also do this indirectly through the conscientious way we work and in the quality of the love and compassion we try to show whenever we turn to God indirectly in the neighbour in need (Matthew 25:31-46). In this way, the morning offering—the most important prayer we make at the beginning of our day—enables us to transform our whole lives into the Mass. By this, I mean we do what Christ did every day he was alive on this earth and what our first Christian forebears did before us. We offer all we say and do to God and receive from him in return the self-same love that Christ received.

We receive this love in return to the measure in which we are prepared to die with him, to all that prevents his loving transforming us into the new High Priest so that the whole of our lives gradually becomes the Mass. In other words, it becomes the place where all we say and do is offered to God in Christ, the New Temple together with all Christians who are now, as St Peter put it, 'A royal priesthood a nation set apart to give glory to God' (1 Peter 2:9). Or, as St Paul puts it, 'Whatever you eat, whatever you drink, whatever you do at all, do it for the glory of God' (1 Corinthians 10:31). In summary, in the words of perhaps the greatest ever liturgical historian Joseph Jungmann SJ, I quote yet again that 'The Mass should so form us that the whole of our lives should become the Mass, the place where we continually offer ourselves through Christ to the Father'.

That is why the first Christians were so aware of their priesthood not ending at Mass but continuing outside of Mass, as all that was said and done was offered to God through Christ. In light of this, my mother told me that by saying my Morning Offering, I would become a little priest, turning ordinary, commonplace things into extraordinary, beautiful acts of love, as Rumpelstiltskin changed straw into gold.

CHAPTER 26

The Way, A Spiritual Journey

CHRISTIANITY WAS ORIGINALLY CALLED a 'Way', or rather, 'The Way'. In other words, it is a journey, an expedition, a great adventure. And it is more exciting, thrilling, engrossing, and ultimately more rewarding than any other conceivable journey. Furthermore, this journey is open to all because it involves falling in love. The more lowly, the more humble a person is, then the greater the possibility that they will succeed. Ultimately, the journey involves falling in love, not with anything nor with any other human being, but with the One who created the world in the first place. St Augustine puts it this way: 'To fall in Love with God is the greatest romance; to seek Him, the greatest adventure; to find Him, the greatest human achievement'. All of us are called to this journey, and the journey begins here and now for those who are prepared to become more than mere nominal Catholics and plunge themselves without delay into the love of God.

God is love. So, when he created us in his own image and likeness, his love dwelt deep down within us. It dwells there not just as the very foundation of our being but as the very centre of our being. Here, it can be experienced in the heart that never ceases to yearn for God despite the sludge of sin and selfishness that tries to stifle it. That is why St Augustine said that our hearts are restless until they rest in God. The more selfless our endeavour, the more our hearts can be open to receive in return, evermore fully, something of the infinite love that can support and sustain it as it yearns to be united with the divine.

All forms of prayer to which we turn—from the very beginning to the heights of mystical union—have one thing in common. They are to help us do one thing: support, strengthen, and sustain the God-given yearning he has placed within us so that it can continually rise to act as a spiritual lightning conductor. This supernatural lightning conductor directs the love of God into the very heart of our being. Here, it suffuses, surcharges, and sustains the only love that can rise to make us one with the One who dwells in love without measure, which is our final destiny. This ongoing and ever-deepening prayer can rise to God only because it takes place within our Risen Lord, where it gradually fuses with his loving of God. The more deeply our prayer is united with Christ's prayer, the faster we journey on, in, with, and through 'The Way', as his love propels us onward in the only journey that really matters.

Anyone setting out on a journey of any magnitude must first make preparations so they will be sustained when alone and bereft of the support they felt at the beginning when initial fervour or enthusiasm inspired them. When we are feeling most lost, vulnerable, and insecure, we can turn to those prayers that we were taught from the beginning. I am referring to prayers like the Our Father, the Hail Mary, the Glory Be, and other prayers, along with hymns, canticles, and psalms we have inherited through hallowed tradition. In trying times, my blueprint for prayer can provide a spiritual backbone, keeping us together and on course when we are in danger of floundering. Therefore, I have expanded on this blueprint in a booklet that I have written for the Catholic Truth Society, 'Prayer Made Simple', and in my book, Never Too Late to Love, and in more detail in my video course on prayer that you will find on the website of Essentialist Press.

However, when we choose to respond to the Holy Spirit, who is always calling us onward into Christ and in him to the Father, Catholic tradition has, from the beginning, taught the way forward for someone prepared to take the next step on the way to loving God the Father. When, at the Last Supper, St Philip asked Christ to show them the Father, Christ asked, 'Do you not believe that I am in the Father, and the Father is in me?' (John 14:10). Now, we can see that in order to begin loving God in himself, we must begin by loving Him as he is present in the human being of his Son, Jesus Christ. This is how the first Apostles began their search for God and how they, in their turn, taught the members of the infant Church to do the same.

With Christianity, a totally new form of preparation for prayer was born, called *meditation*. However, unlike previous or contemporary forms of meditation, it was not centred on themselves. Instead, it was centred on God and on his love as it was first embodied in Jesus Christ and in all he said and did. The love generated there will enable us to enter into Christ as he is now in his Risen glory. So, as we have seen, love of its very nature yearns for union. As St Augustine insists, the deep yearning in all of us will be satisfied and consummated only when it rests in God.

The love generated from coming to know and love Jesus Christ then, as he once was, through daily meditation, is the only love that can enable us to come to know and love him as he is now, . By this, I mean as he is now in his Mystical Body. Then, from being drawn up into his mystical human being, we are taken up into his mystical human action. That means into his mystical loving of his Father. As we participate with him in his sublime contemplation of his Father, we receive the fruits of contemplation in return. These fruits are the infused virtues, the fruits and gifts of the Holy Spirit that can not only change us but, through us, can change the world in which we live.

For centuries, the Mystical Theology teaching how this love is purified so we unite ourselves with Christ has been forgotten and even derided by those who should know better. G.K. Chesterton said, 'The Christian ideal has not been tried and found wanting. It has been found difficult and so left untried'. St Paul said that he preached Christ and him crucified, and anyone who is not prepared to take up their daily cross as this journey progresses will never be able to rise with Christ to be united with the One for whom they have been thirsting from the beginning.

CHAPTER 27

Christ's Own Contemplation

ALTHOUGH IT IS IMPERATIVE that all of Christendom must turn back to prayer and without delay, no one seems to be listening. Our Lady has been begging us to do this for years, but nobody seems to be hearing her. After her appearances, pilgrims in their hundreds of thousands rushed out to where she appeared to see the place for themselves. They wanted to meet those who witnessed the appearances, to speak with them, to touch them. They wanted to see miracles, the sun dancing in the sky, witness healings, and have their personal prayers and petitions answered. But how many listen to her message, which is not about how to have or see esoteric experiences but how to pray in order to come to know and love her Son?

I have already explained how The Talmud shows how Jewish mothers and fathers like Our Lady and St Joseph would have taught their Son how to pray each day from morning to night. I have also shown how, in the early Church, these prayers were Christianised by our first spiritual ancestors. However, in addition to this mainly vocal prayer, another deeper form of prayer called *meditation* was introduced. It was introduced in order to enable a person to enter into Christ and then into his contemplation of his Father. Because Christ was without sin, he could contemplate his Father's love at every moment of his life on earth. This contemplation enabled him to receive the fruits of contemplation contained within the love he received from his Father, as all the colours of the spectrum are contained within a single shaft of light.

In this way, the Risen Christ became a supernatural prism God could use to channel his love through his Son to the world. At first, and because his human being was restricted to a certain part of the world at a certain time in history, only a limited number of people could benefit from his love. However, after his glorification, his human body was transformed into a Mystical Body, transcending space and time restrictions. Consequently, his love could be transmitted to everyone at every moment in history, at any time and in any place. However, as those of us who wish to receive this love and its supernatural gifts are not immaculately conceived, we must undergo a second baptism of fire. In this baptism, the Holy Spirit purifies and so prepares us to receive the fruits of divine love that Christ received before us, enabling us to do for others in our day what Christ did in his day.

Although, at baptism, everyone is taken up into Christ's Mystical Body, the Holy Spirit draws all who would follow his powerful magnetic love further and deeper into the glorified Christ. This means that we will not only be able to share in his new life, but also into his action, —into his loving of his Father. This same loving enabled him to be open to his Father's love whilst he was on earth but in a new and even more powerful way. Firstly, because after his Ascension into heaven, the mutual loving that bound him to his Father whilst he was on earth, was intensified by his transformed and transfigured body and soul, that would redetermine his close and intimate relationship with his Father. Secondly, because all who are drawn up into him after baptism can now not only share in this sublime new relationship, but even in the mutual contemplative loving that now bonds the glorified Christ to his Father. However, as those who are now called to take part in this mutual loving with his Father are not immaculately conceived, there will always need to be a profound inner purification before their ultimate hopes and dreams can be realised. This realisation and the practical experience of what this purification involves is responsible for the vast majority who give up after beginning this journey. St John of the Cross said that ninety percent of those who come to the beginning of purification run away.

Those who run away from the purgatorial purification that is offered in this life might console themselves with their ultimate salvation in the next life, thanks to purgatory. But they will not be able to work effectively for the salvation and sanctification of others in this life, which they have been called to do at Baptism. Far more persevered in the early Church, thanks to the teaching and example of the Apostles who preached Christ and him crucified. Furthermore, they encouraged their followers to take up their daily cross inside as well as outside of prayer. In this way, they were prepared to rise with Christ and also to enter into him and into his transcendent loving or his Mystical Contemplation of God the Father. Only then can they observe the First Commandment like never before, as they participate in Christ's own loving of his Father. This sublime, wordless, all-engrossing, all-consuming loving of his Father is called his hidden or Mystical Contemplation.

Only by being drawn up and into his Mystical Contemplation will we gradually begin to receive, in ever deeper, ever fuller measure, the fruits of Contemplation, enabling us to do for others in our world what Christ did for others in his world over two thousand years ago. If we read the Gospels, we can see just what Christ was able to do in the Jewish world into which he was born. If we read the Acts of the Apostles, we will be able to see what his followers were able to do in the Roman world in which they spread the Good News.

What they did can be done again by those who are prepared to journey on in 'The Way' where they will be so purified that they will be led into the contemplation of our Risen Lord, to receive the fruits of contemplation that can make the impossible possible, as it did over two thousand years ago. Remember those memorable words of St Thomas Aquinas, 'To contemplate and to share the fruits of our contemplation with others'. Doing this in, with, and through Christ is the very essence of the God-given spirituality that Christ introduced into the early Church. It is the spirituality to which we must return without delay; without it, the renewal for which we are still awaiting will continue to evade us.

CHAPTER 28

Into the Sacred Heart

IF YOU ARE TRAVELLING to a distant destination, you will have to travel by car or coach, by train or plane, by ship or spaceship. The spiritual journey is much the same. This journey has an infinite destination because it is into the Love of God, which never ends this side of eternity. The journey also requires a special 'vehicle'—, the human person of Jesus Christ who has already completed the journey before us. He knows the way because he is 'The Way'. It is not just human energy alone that will enable us to enter into him; something more is required. This extra something is the love that Christ himself released on the first Pentecost Day after completing his own journey.

Those who chose to receive this love and continue choosing to receive it through their baptism are drawn up into Christ's own personal Mystical Body, which now spans the distance between heaven and earth. However, at the centre of this Mystical Body is a Sacred Heart. This Sacred Heart is like a supernatural engine that enables the love of Christ to continually rise into God and also those who have been drawn into his loving Sacred Heart to rise with him. But those who would rise in, with, and through him must first be prepared through a deep personal purification, for imperfect human hearts cannot be united with the perfect Sacred Heart of Jesus. As this purification deepens, it will enable a human heart to be one with his heart in being and in loving, enabling it to rise in, with, and through him, and at speed, to the Father.

There is then only one thing necessary for this journey: love. Firstly, this means the perfect love of Christ; secondly, it means our imperfect love has to be made sufficiently perfect to be united with his love. This purification is brought about in meditation and then in contemplation. This point is so important that I must explain myself further. The Apostles, the first disciples, and all the new converts who were received into the early Church first and foremost had to meet Christ personally, come to love him, and then have their love purified in such a way that they could enter into him. In this singular way, they could be made one with his loving, which could alone enable their loving then and our loving now to be united with God.

It was for this reason, the very first thing the apostles taught new converts was to come to know and love Jesus Christ as they had come to know and love him when he was on earth. It would be in this way, a similar human love that had drawn them to him whilst he was on earth would draw them to him, too. A new form of preparation for prayer was therefore developed. In this new approach to prayer, that came to be called *meditation*, a beginner who had never met Christ in person could meet him in their hearts and minds that would be set afire by the memories of those who had come to know and love him in person while he was alive on earth. Often, two or even three Apostles or disciples who had known Christ personally would electrify their listeners at the weekly Eucharist or around the fireside, where, for centuries, tales of the past had been told to inspire future generations. Their listeners would be encouraged to reflect and ruminate on these stories in personal meditation, generating the love that would fill them with a desire to be united with the One they had come to know and love. If you read the earliest sources, you will find that the Christians who were taught to pray five or six times a day were encouraged to use this time to meditate on the life, death, and Resurrection of Christ, too. Like the Apostles before them, they would come to know and love him as he once was before his death and Resurrection. This relationship would become the spiritual stepping stone to loving him as he is now, where the union they crave above all else could be realised.

However, although it is possible to love someone who once lived but who no longer lives on earth, it is not possible to be united with them. Here, at the critical point in a person's spiritual journey that a change of direction takes place, which is the special prerogative of the Holy Spirit. The love that is generated in meditation is now redirected from the Christ who once lived on earth to the Christ who now lives in heaven. This shift is what happened to the first Apostles and the earliest disciples and is the same transference they desired for their first spiritual sons and daughters. Once this occurred, then, like them, they too could be united in love with the Risen and glorified Lord and through him with his Father. That is why they developed this new form of preparation for prayer, that, eventually came to be called *meditation*.

I have already shown how the first apostles, like St Paul after his conversion, spent many years in prayer after they had received the Holy Spirit. They did this so the Holy Spirit could purify their imperfect love of Christ in such a way that they would not only enable that love to be taken up into Christ's Mystical Body but into his pure mystical loving of his Father through his Sacred Heart. This process was essential because it was only in sharing in Christ's mystical loving, his Mystical Contemplation, that they would receive all the fruits of contemplation. This reception would enable them to share these fruits with others through their apostolic endeavour that would take them all over the known world. Alone, they could not convert a pagan Empire into a Christian Empire, and that is why they taught all new converts the way through meditation to contemplation so that the fruits of the Holy Spirit could work through them, too, to do what was quite impossible without him.

Sadly, when after over three hundred years or more, the pagan Roman Empire had become a Christian Empire, laxity began to creep in, and the profound Mystical Spirituality that had animated the early Church soon became the way for the few, not for the many as it had been in the early Church. All renewal that did subsequently renew the Church came through the great saints and mystics who returned to the profound Mystical Prayer that animated our first Christian forebears. Any objective observer will see that not just the world but even our beloved Church is enveloped by an unwelcome and anti-Christian moral morass.

This chaos can be overcome only by returning without delay to the spirituality of our first Christian ancestors. The Holy Spirit is ready to lead and guide us as he led and guided our first spiritual ancestors. Yet, are we ready to let him? What follows will be the traditional teaching of the great apostles, saints, and mystics who have detailed how to cooperate with the only One who can lead us back into Christ and into his love and ultimately back to the Father.

CHAPTER 29

Beginning the Journey

JONATHAN SWIFT, THE AUTHOR of *Gulliver's Travels,* said that we have just enough religion to make us hate but not enough to make us love one another. It is for this reason that we must return to the sources of our religion to discover and steep ourselves in the love that was the heart and soul of early Christian Spirituality. I am not primarily talking about human love but about the divine love that was to be found in the person of Jesus Christ, who totally dominated the minds and hearts of everyone who called themselves Christians.

If everyone who was proud to call themselves Christians today made this journey back to their first beginnings, then we would all find ourselves unified because we would all be transformed by the Love of Christ. This transformation would make us one with him and in him so that our hearts and our minds would synchronise with his heart and mind, making us one with him and with one another. Beginners who sought to be admitted to the new religion based on love were not promptly bombarded with a plethora of Catechetical teaching, nor did they have to learn creeds by heart or commit catechisms to memory, at least to begin with. Firstly, and above all else, they were directed to the heart and soul of God's love that was to be found, as the Apostles had found it, embodied in the person of Jesus Christ during his life on earth.

As the first Christians still rigorously observed the Ten Commandments, Jesus Christ could not be physically depicted in any shape or form. Therefore, from the very beginning, those who joined the new religion were taught how to picture their new Lord in their mind's eye, in their imaginations, and from the memories of those who knew him. This imagining prepared them for the prayer called *meditation*. (This word was not initially used since meditation at the time typically described the rhythmic mantras—used by Gurus from India and Gnostics, and later, Neoplatonists from Europe—to generate inner psychological states of wellbeing.) Once it was clear that Christian meditation was instead used to generate the human love of the most loveable and adorable human being who had ever walked on the face of this earth, things changed.

In subsequent centuries, the word was used to designate the starting point for those who wished not just to love the Christ who once lived but the Christ who still lives amongst us by leading us into his own Mystical Contemplation. At this point, I can almost hear my readers sighing, saying to themselves, *what a pity that is not for me*. That this sort of prayer that constitutes the journey to union with God is not for the laity is outrageous and the consequence of a massive historical misconception responsible for the present state of spiritual stagnation currently starving the faithful. They seem to think that the profound mystical journey that enabled the first Christians to be drawn up through Christ into the love that unites him with his Father, was only for monks in their monasteries or nuns in their nunneries or mendicants in their friaries or priories. Monks did not exist in Christendom for several hundred years after Christ rose from the dead, and mendicants like Dominicans, Franciscans, and Carmelites did not exist for almost a millennium after them. The early Christian spirituality that set the world on fire in those early centuries was embodied in those who practised the daily meditation that led to Mystical Contemplation.

It was lay people's spirituality that began, advanced, prospered and was brought to perfection in the family, as I have laboured to emphasize and will continue to emphasise. Although there were a few men and women who chose to embrace a celibate life, it was primarily laypeople who transmitted to the world the God-given spirituality that Christ had given them, transforming the pagan world in such a short period of time. This transformation was not primarily the work of men and women but of Christ and his love that worked in and through them to do what could not possibly be achieved by human endeavour alone. The very essence of their spirituality consisted in firstly developing human love—by loving the person of Jesus Christ as the first Apostles came to know and love him before them. When it seemed that he was taken away from them, their love for him had to be purified in a way that had not been expected at the beginning of the journey.

Although they knew that the Holy Spirit had taken them up at Pentecost into their beloved Lord, his presence was not tangible as it was before. The reason for this was simple. Unlike their Lord (and his blessed mother, who was still with them), they had not been immaculately conceived; this is painfully obvious to anyone who studies their behaviour before Pentecost. In order to enter into Christ's Sacred Heart and thence into his sacred loving of his Father, their love had to be systematically purified like all the other mystics and saints who would come after them. This purification took time because there is no such thing as instant sanctity. What was true for the Apostles and their first disciples is true for us; it is best to realise this from the beginning.

Once a person is totally committed to daily meditation, this preparation for contemplation rarely lasts for more than two to three years. (Interestingly enough, this is about the same amount of time, that the apostles experienced Christ's physical presence amongst them.) What happens next is what happened to the Apostles. The

Holy Spirit takes the initiative by raising them up and into the Mystical Body of Christ. Here, their desire to love God persists, although the presence of his physical body that they had come to see, love, and experience in their minds by using their reason, their imaginations, and their memory disappears from their prayer life for a long time—perhaps permanently in this life. The time for meditation is over; time for contemplation has begun. In a lifetime given up to meditation and contemplation, only a comparative fraction of the time is given up to meditation; the rest is given up to contemplation. It is, therefore, essential that we know what *contemplation* means. It means *to gaze with loving intent on something or someone*. The Romantic poets describe what it means (or rather feels like) to contemplate the 'numinous 'or the transcendent in the beauty of creation. This is sometimes called *natural contemplation*.

In Christian meditation, we eventually learn to gaze at the beauty of the masterwork of creation, Jesus Christ, in what has been called *Acquired Contemplation*. In what later came to be called *Mystical Contemplation*, we come to gaze upon the beauty or the glory of the creator of all creation, in, with, through and together with the masterwork of creation—namely, Jesus Christ.

The sort of purification necessary to be united with Christ so as to be one with him in his Mystical Contemplation of his Father is not required of those who come to experience natural or Acquired contemplation. Thus, I must now turn our attention to what is effectively the purgatory on earth that can alone unite us with Christ in such a way that, through him, we can come to contemplate the glory of God. The more fully all Christians are united together in Christ in this sublime action, the sooner their religion will unite them in the love that will extinguish the hatred that has historically separated them from each other with terrible consequences.

CHAPTER 30

The Meaning of Mystical Contemplation

AFTER LAXITY BEGUN TO SEEP into the Church once Christianity had been made the official religion of the Roman Empire, the Church turned to monasticism for help to renew herself. Although monks (particularly the Irish monks) initially excelled in holiness, as the centuries rolled by, they too fell into decline. This decline was not so much in their monasteries but in the world where they began to linger for too long away from the spirituality that had formed them. When itinerant monks began to give scandal to others after they had lost their way, it was time for authority to step in.

Shortly after his coronation as the Holy Roman Emperor on Christmas Day in 800 AD, Charlemagne not only ordered all such monks back to their monasteries but also insisted that all monasteries in his empire adopt the Benedictine rule. Although the vow of stability ensured there would no longer be bad monks doing harm, it also meant there would no longer be good monks doing good. This shift meant that until the mendicant orders came in the thirteenth century, ordinary Catholics lacked the constant spiritual help and support they needed. They were called *mendicant orders* from the Latin word meaning *beggars*. Mendicant friars had no time to support themselves, giving all their time to contemplation when they were at home in their priories and friaries and all their time preaching and teaching when they were away from home. Consequently, they

130

looked to the laity to whose spiritual wellbeing they had committed themselves, for financial help.

I cannot help thinking that it was a certain amount of jealously on the part of malcontented monks, who looked with some envy on the freedom given to mendicant friars. Some of them complained, insisting that the mendicants should return to their friaries and priories to practise contemplation there. It was precisely to answer these criticisms that in defence of the new mendicant orders (the Dominicans, the Franciscans, the Carmelites and the Augustinians), St Thomas Aquinas uttered his famous retort: 'Our work is to contemplate and then to share the fruits of contemplation with others'. In other words, just as contemplation is the heart and soul of the monastic life, it is likewise the heart and soul of their mendicant life, St Thomas insisted, as it should be for the life of the Church, as it was from the very beginning.

He explained that they were trying to follow in the footsteps of the first apostles, going out into the world to share with others the fruits of their contemplation, which alone would empower them to bring about God's kingdom in the world. To do this outside the spiritual security of their monastic seclusion, they had to give more time to the personal prayer that leads to contemplation inside their priories, friaries and hermitages. As we will see more clearly later, the method of prayer used by a person who has been led into contemplation is the best possible form of prayer for a person called to live and work in the world precisely because it is so simple.

The word *contemplation* is so important that I would now like to give it back its original meaning. In general, the word means *to gaze in awe at someone or something*, but Christian contemplation means *to gaze in awe upon the creator of all things, in and together with Jesus Christ, here and now in his risen glory*. The journey upon which we have embarked is a journey into Christ so that, in him, surcharged with the love that is generated by his Sacred heart, our loving is purified by his loving. It is so purified that the two loves become as one, enabling our heartbeats to synchronise with his heartbeat, rising as one to be embraced, enveloped, and then embodied in God. Christian contemplation is human loving raised to a higher supernatural level by being subsumed into the loving of Christ, not just making it possible for us to rise in such a way that our love can enter into God, but for his love to descend and enter into us.

Unlike Christ, who was at all times able to give and receive perfect love to his Father in unsullied Mystical Contemplation, our servitude to self prevents us from doing what our restless hearts wish to do more than anything else. For this reason, the first apostles preached Christ and, as St Paul put it, 'Christ crucified' because in order for us to be freed from servitude to self, we have to take up our daily cross and follow him, daily dying to self both inside and outside of prayer.

By teaching the faithful to meditate on the person of Christ, the first apostles who had known him were able to see what continual contemplation did for him. It endowed him with the fruits of contemplation, with all the love that generated the infused virtues and the gifts of the Holy Spirit that enabled them to see in him what God wanted to do in them. To put it another way, the apostles wanted them to see through their meditation the perfect human being whom they would be inspired to emulate. But that was not all. They wanted the love that would be generated by their meditation to be redirected by the Holy Spirit, from the Christ who once lived in history to the Christ who now lives in Majesty. The union, which is the deepest desire of all lovers, can only take place between two people who are alive and living now.

I have already shown how, after Pentecost, the apostles spent many years in profound contemplative prayer, being purified to be fully reunited with their Risen Lord. This purification involved the daily dying to self that would enable them to receive the fruits of contemplation, without which they could not have converted the many thousands of people who would become the foundation of the Church. They, in their turn, would inspire new converts by the fruits of contemplation that were clearly embodied in them. Through Mystical Contemplation and through the fruits of contemplative loving, the greatest mass conversion the world had ever known took place.

In defining the vocation of the Dominican Order, St Thomas was also defining the vocation of every other Order. Furthermore, he was defining the vocation of the Church, not just in ancient times but for all times. That is why in his massive masterwork, *The Three Ages of the Interior Life*, the Dominican Fr Reginald Garrigou-Lagrange (perhaps the greatest spiritual theologian of modern times) insisted that contemplation is for all. As we shall soon see, and contrary to expectations, it is the simplest form of prayer. Yet, one of the greatest contemporary Church scandals is the ongoing movement not to suppress only contemplative prayer but also the monasteries, the priories, the convents, and the religious houses where this prayer is deemed the ideal. The latest iconoclasts are pseudo-intellectuals and pseudo-Christians, who think, like the Gnostics who preceded them, that the faith is not primarily about love but about knowledge. By *knowledge,* I mean their particular brand of woke and worldly knowledge, with which they want to pervert the faith of our Fathers in order to change the world, not into the image and likeness of Christ, but of the anti-Christ who they now represent.

CHAPTER 31

The Mass and Mystical Prayer

THE WORD *ENTHUSIASM* comes from Greek, meaning *to be wrapped in God*. The first part of the spiritual adventure we have embarked on leads us onward to be wrapped in God when meditation reaches its climax. But this is only the first enthusiasm that reaches its high point in what I have called *Acquired Contemplation*. Enthusiasm is brought to perfection when a person is finally wrapped in God in what traditional Mystical Theology from the time of St Bernard has called the *Mystical Marriage*.

When Meditation has led the searcher into contemplation, prolonged periods of purification in spiritual darkness are interspersed with moments of light and enlightenment. The ensuing moments of mystical enthusiasm that follow are called by St Teresa of Avila the 'Prayer of Quiet' or even the 'Prayer of Full Union'. These moments of spiritual transportations into the love of God are his gifts and can never be attained, let alone merited merely by human endeavour. This uncontrollable nature is made quite evident by the unpredictable and capricious way they come and go without anything the receiver can do to generate or retain them. Nor are they given as a reward for perseverance, but rather to encourage the sort of perseverance in the journey toward the Mystical Marriage when we are completely wrapped in the love of God.

But I am getting ahead of myself. Let me return to the meditation that leads to the climax of first enthusiasm. The journey begins because of the love that rises from within us, that, as St Augustine says, will be ever restless until it rests in God. Because we begin our journey not wrapped in God but rather in ourselves. Therefore, this love that yearns for God is waylaid with a thousand and one other lesser loves that would distract it from its purpose. By their own endeavour alone, no one can extricate themselves from all the powerful forces within. These would distract and prevent the love that they wish to be wrapped up in God, being wrapped up in themselves instead. Only the love of God can do the impossible, which is why what I call the 'Asceticism of the Heart' has a simple objective. It does not attempt to free us from all that prevents our heart's desire from rising to God but only to keep our heart's desire fixed on God, despite the distractions and temptations that would prevent it.

This practice alone will gradually create a mystical pathway that will enable our love to rise to God and also his love to descend into us. It is His love and his love alone that can destroy within us everything currently preventing us from coming to know and love him as we desire with every fibre of our being. Therefore, we must always do all we can to keep our heart's desire—our love—directed toward God, whom we desire before all else. This directing of love is what Christ himself did throughout his life on earth. Christ's love from within continually rose up to reach out to and into his Father at all times. Nevertheless, like us, he had to bear distractions and temptations too. Unlike us, these distractions did not come from the Original Sin, which was never in him. It came from the Original Sin that was in others who wanted to destroy him. Before going any further in describing the spiritual journey that is ahead of us, let me make it quite clear that we are not making this journey only in Christ since, by Baptism, we have been taken up and into him, but we are making it in, with, and through him.

Firstly, realise that the more we come to know and love him in meditation and contemplation, the more perfectly we are united with him, enabling us to travel with ever greater speed toward the destiny that God has prepared for us. Secondly, realise that the essential offering we make to God in our journey is exactly the same offering Christ made throughout his life on earth. In other words, we are offering to God our love, as Christ offered to God his love. Christ called this offering the new worship 'in spirit and in truth'. In short, this is how we take up and carry our cross in our daily prayer as the first Christians did in their daily prayer. Therefore, far from being an extraordinary way for the few, the way that I am describing is for all. It is not just one way amongst many others, but 'The Way', the only way we practise what the early Christians called 'white martyrdom', or the daily way of the cross.

In all our daily prayers, and in the meditation and the contemplation I am trying to explain, deep down beneath the surface of everything else, is the offering. It is the same sort of offering that Christ himself made every day of his life. In other words, it is the offering of the sacrifice of our hearts, our love to God the Father. At the Last Supper, this living sacrifice of himself that reached its climax on the Cross was celebrated in what eventually came to be called the sacrifice of the Mass, when all the offerings of a lifetime were embodied in a profound liturgical action. This liturgical action would embody both his struggle against the forces of evil directed at him throughout his life on earth and with his continual contemplation of his Father, which was brought to perfection after his Resurrection. At Mass, the fruits of his contemplation are continually being poured out to be received by those who participate in this sublime mystery, but only to the measure of their openness to receive them. This openness to receive the gifts and fruits of contemplation that he received will be determined by the quality of a receiver's union with Christ.

The journey I am describing into Christ and into his contemplation of his Father is not some mystical ego trip for weirdos. It is the way in which our love is gradually reinforced, deepened, purified, and refined so that it can be united with the Sacrifice that Christ made for us while he was on earth and continues to make for us now that he is in heaven.

The measure of our capacity to receive God's love that is continually pouring into him in this sublime sacrament will be determined by the measure in which we are able to make our whole lives into the Mass. Our lives become the Mass when we follow Christ by living our lives as he did—by being continually open to God at all times despite all the evil forces that endeavour to turn our attention elsewhere. This is our vocation. As we are about to see, it is a vocation first practised in prayer through meditation, where our love is first generated. Then it proceeds through contemplation, where it is finally purified, enabling us to be wrapped in God, where our first enthusiasm reaches its consummation in the Mystical Marriage that begins in this life and never ends in the next.

CHAPTER 32

How to Practise Catholic Meditation

LONG BEFORE TELEVISION, I became addicted to the radio, or *the wireless* as we called it then. My favourite programme for children was called 'How Things Began'. It featured Uncle Jim, who would take young listeners with him back into the past. We would see and experience for ourselves how the world was created, how life first began in the sea, how the first creature to populate the land arose from the ocean and grew into terrible lizards or Dinosaurs. Then, we would see for ourselves how the first mammals emerged, how the first men and women were born and how they spread all over the world, and how the past still influences the world we live in. He used to say, 'Open your eyes and see, open your ears and hear, open your noses and smell. You must so immerse yourself in the past that it becomes as the present. Then use your minds to understand what you see, and you will be able to make history real in a way that you will be able to apprehend it like never before'.

Thanks to Uncle Jim, when the principle and purpose of meditation were explained to me, I was able to go back into the past as he taught me. But this time, not to see and understand the beginnings of the physical world, but to see and understand the beginnings of the Christian world. I was there when Christ was born. I saw it with my own inner eyes. I heard what Mary and Joseph said, what the shepherds and the three kings exclaimed, and why they suddenly had to make a dash for Egypt to live in exile until Herod was dead. I visited Nazareth when Jesus was growing up, but most importantly of all, I was there when he was baptised in the river Jordan. I followed him throughout his life on earth, listening to what he had to say and watching how people reacted to him, especially when out, of unprecedented care and compassion, he healed the sick and the dying and even raised the dead.

Looking back, I can now see that I was in the best possible predicament to move forward and move forward at speed in the great spiritual adventure that would enthral me for the rest of my life. As I was a boarder in the sixth form, I had a whole hour after supper and before night prayers to practise meditation, although twenty minutes was enough to begin with. As I had only just decided that I wanted to become a priest, it was too late for me to begin studying Greek even if I did not suffer from dyslexia, so instead, I studied scripture. Scripture study not only enabled me to become a bystander in the main events in Christ's life, but it also enabled me to understand more deeply the significance of what I saw and heard. Without meditation, I would have had no future because when I entered the Franciscan novitiate with little Latin and still with reading and writing difficulties due to my dyslexia, what others seemed to enjoy became a living hell for me. However, every evening after Compline and before bed, I had plenty of time to escape into the world where I could come to know and love ever more deeply the person of Jesus Christ as he lived and loved in our world before the Resurrection.

It was about Easter time, when my meditation came to a climax. Throughout Lent, I had been beguiled by the profound mystical teaching of Jesus during the Last Supper. Then, after I heard and assimilated what he said as I imagined myself sitting with him at the same table as the Apostles, all my inner faculties were raised to a state of high emotional intensity. It was not just that he said he wanted us to be his friends, but even more than that. He wanted us to be united with him in such a way that he could make his home in us, and we could make our home in him. So, with him all things would become possible, even the impossible, as I had been able to visualise him performing the impossible throughout his time on earth. What finally moved me more than anything else was how the world—which he had come to teach how to love and how to create a new world in which goodness, truth and unity would prevail where evil, error, and anarchy had prevailed before—simply rejected him. They not only rejected him, but they hated him for it. When my meditation followed him from the Upper Room and into the Garden of Gethsemane, I saw for myself as I prayed with the Apostles the terrible toll that his approaching passion and death was having upon him.

Unlike the Apostles, I knew what was coming next. I knew too what made him sweat blood: not just the atrocities he would have to endure but also what little effect his suffering would have on the world for which he was prepared to give his all, and in such an appalling way. It was perhaps not so much hatred for what he represented that added to his suffering but apathy and indifference. I vowed that I would not desert him. Using all the inner human resources available to me from my memory, my imagination, and my mind with its powers of reasoning and understanding, I tried to remain faithful. I was there in spirit, in mind, and in heart, amongst the soldiers with the bystanders as Jesus was first scourged, crowned with thorns and then ridiculed by drunken louts. I followed in my mind and in my imagination over many weeks as he carried his Cross all the way to Calvary. I was there too when, in pitch darkness, he was taken down from the Cross and laid in the sepulchre.

At this point, my human love for the love of God in Jesus Christ reached its climax as I meditated on his Resurrection and reflected on all that had led up to this dramatic otherworldly climax. All I wanted to do day after day was to gaze upon him now in his risen glory. All I wanted to do was to gaze upon him without any words. All had been said; all had been seen; all had been reflected upon. All I wanted to do was to gaze in a profound contemplative stillness on the One who had done so much, not just for the world in general, but for me in particular. I had arrived at what has been called *Acquired Contemplation* at the height of meditation. Like so many others, I thought I had arrived at the height of the Mystic Way. But I would have to think again when suddenly the sweet, all-absorbing prayer that enveloped me suddenly came to an end, never to return, at least not in quite the same way.

Although I did not know it at the time, God had heard the prayer I had been making, and he answered it by leading me into true Mystical Contemplation, although, at the time, it felt more like purgatory on earth than anything else. At least, that's what I thought at the time, and I was right!

CHAPTER 33

Loving the Christ of History, to Union with Christ in Majesty

MY COMPARATIVE SUCCESS in my prayer life, and in such a short time, deceived me as it would deceive many others into believing I had arrived at what the great saints and mystics call the *Mystical Marriage* or the *Transforming Union*. I had, in fact, only arrived at the heights of first enthusiasm or first fervour. Without help in taking the next step in the great adventure that had come to a critical crossroads, I could spend months, even years, going around in circles, provided that I did not give up the journey altogether. Just because what I have been describing as first fervour comes to an end when we are called into the Mystic Way, does not mean that this stage of the spiritual adventure is pointless or insignificant. On the contrary, it is of vital importance, just as the honeymoon period in human love is of vital importance to the whole journey into perfect love. What happens in meditation, we first discover God's love in the person of Jesus Christ. That is why he came—and that is why God's Son was made flesh and dwelt amongst us—so that other human beings of flesh and blood could first discover God's love in the flesh and blood of Jesus Christ.

What happens in meditation is that, ideally, the yearning for God, the restless desire to rest in him that was initially so weak and fragile though real, is deepened, sharpened, and brought almost to a fever pitch. This is not an artificial love or generated in a fantasy world of our own making. It is inspired by the Holy Spirit, who inspired the scriptures in the first place so that we could learn of God's love, found in his Son, Jesus Christ. The weak and tender love that led us into meditation then grows and deepens and then finally reaches a climax. In this climax, our love for Christ, like all genuine love, begins to desire not just to be close to him—to be near him continuously—but to enter into him. All love wants is to be united with the one who is loved, not just for some of the time but for all of the time.

This desire is precisely what happens at the climax of Acquired Contemplation. The love that was once no more than a gentle pull towards God now becomes like an uncontrollable craving for union with Christ and the One who lives in him. As we have seen before, although it is not impossible to love someone who once lived on this earth, it is impossible to be united with them, no matter how strong that love is. Fortunately, what I have called the *yearning for God*, the craving to be one with him that is experienced at the heights of first fervour, is rightly understood by the Holy Spirit as a prayer for the union for which God initially created us. Inevitably, then, and in every case, our prayer is answered. The Holy Spirit leads us out of meditation and into contemplation, where something vital and indispensable must occur before our deepest desire and longing for union can be satisfied.

Firstly, our love must be redirected to Christ, not as he once was on earth, but as he is now in heaven in his risen glory where the union we desire can take place. Furthermore, it can occur here and now in this life, although it will only be in the next life that this union can be brought to perfection. Secondly (this is why the contemplation that will enable us to be taken up into our Risen Lord is initially so dark), we must undergo a prolonged and all-consuming purification. How can we, as we are, despite our desire for God that has been set alight in meditation, be united with him until a long and testing purification sufficiently prepares us for mystical union? In meditation, we are inspired to follow Christ and be united with him, but in contemplation, we are purified to make possible what is totally impossible without purification. Namely, by endlessly journeying on in practising the simple unadulterated and unconditional loving that can alone unite us with the simple unadulterated and unconditional loving of God himself and his Son, Jesus Christ.

In my last years at school, I was chosen to take part in a Shakespearean anthology in which I was to recite the famous speech of Henry V: 'Once more unto the breach, dear friends, once more ...' The rehearsal was a flop and the English master saw it, although he said not a word. Minutes before the curtain rose, he took me aside and delivered a speech of his own that so inspired me with love for the man whom I was about to portray that he turned what would otherwise have been a terrible tragedy into a roaring success. I no longer floundered around the stage, making flamboyant and fanciful gestures that I had practised before a full-length mirror, believing I was genuinely imitating the man I had been asked to portray. Suddenly, and thanks to the English master, I became the greatest warrior-king in English history. Why? Because I was animated from within by the same spirit that had inspired the king who trounced the French at Agincourt.

This genuineness is what gradually happens in contemplation. In meditation, we are inspired by Christ but from the outside. So, when we try to imitate him, it can seem rather contrived and artificial, as my first attempt to play the part of Henry had been at the rehearsal. But in contemplation, we learn how to imitate Christ from the inside by learning how to open ourselves continually to the self-same love he received from his Father during his life on earth. To receive this love that at all times animated him, we, like him, must learn to face up to and turn away from the same evil that was hurled against him by the sinners who hated him. Furthermore, we must face up to the sinner within us and, through purification, enable the love that at all times animated him to destroy this evil at its source within the nether regions of our personality.

Only then will God's love—the Holy Spirit who inspired and animated him throughout his life on earth—begin to do the same for us. Only the deep purification that takes place in contemplation will enable us to receive the Holy Spirit, as he did, finally enabling us to be united with him not just symbolically but in reality. We shall receive the Holy Spirit not just in his new and risen body but in his new and risen body, soul and divinity and with the love that endlessly rises from his Sacred Heart. Then, to the degree and to the measure that our contemplation is united with his contemplation, we will be able to receive the fruits of contemplation. In this way, Christ will be able to live again and love again in the world that he came to save from the slavery of selfishness and sin through those who choose to receive him and to the end of time.

CHAPTER 34

Prayer and the Charismatic Movement

A RARE AND ANCIENT BOOK on Mystical Theology that was so small and dishevelled that the censors must have overlooked it in the novitiate library gave me the advice I needed. 'When sweet meditation leads you into dark contemplation,' it said, 'be sure that you give to your new prayer exactly the same time as you gave to the preceding prayer'. It is easy to love when all seems sweetness and light, but true love is revealed, deepened, and brought to perfection when you receive nothing in return and are prepared to go on loving. The author insisted that although in human love, even the most true and persistent loving can be rejected, as I had already found to my cost, the contrary is true in Divine love. God never rejects such love and always returns it once its quality has been tried and tested.

For the next two years, I continually gave the same time to the prayer that at least half of that time was dark and gloomy and filled with distractions and temptations—the strongest of which was to cut and run. Although little seemed to have changed in the second year, I gradually came to realize that although I no longer relished prayer as before, I knew that, in some mysterious way, I received strength from my persistence. There were times in the last six months of my sojourn in this spiritual desert when I became aware of a sort of indefinable presence. These experiences were similar to those about which the romantic poets wrote, but I experienced them in a dark church and in a dark soul far from the natural beauty that inspired the poets.

Then, suddenly and without any warning, the subtle experience I had felt for some of the time rose to a degree of intensity that convinced me I was experiencing the love of God. As if to ensure that I could never doubt it, this experience rose on occasions to such a high degree that I believed I was on the boundary of human consciousness. I have described how I found help and encouragement elsewhere in my books; therefore, I will say no more here except one thing. I have said as much as I intend to say to encourage readers onward in what St John of the Cross calls *The Dark Night of the Soul,* and as we will see with what came next in my spiritual journey, that gave me an insight into early Christianity that I want to share with you.

What did come next was that, even before the Second Vatican Council occurred a movement that was sweeping across Europe swept into our student house, converting even the most sceptical, including me, to what was called the 'New Biblical Theology.' It was a theological experience that in some way paralleled in the classroom the mystical experience I had just undergone in the Church. The rather dull, dry, intellectual scholastic theology underpinned with abstract, abstruse Greek philosophy suddenly seemed to be superseded as black-and-white movies were superseded by technicolour. Vivid, colourful pictures, stories, and divine plans and promises were all seen as they were consummated in Christ and in the new God-given spirituality he bequeathed to the early Church. Compared to the highly intellectual theology in which everything had to be defined, divided, and dissected, the 'New Biblical Theology' was much more real, human, and all-absorbing. The Old Testament was seen as full of meaning, as the prequel to the New Testament, where it found its spiritual consummation and ultimate meaning in the person of Christ and in the liturgies that inspired and galvanised the early Christian communities.

This new theology aroused my fellow students from their intellectual torpor and filled them with a new enthusiasm for their faith and for the way it was expressed in the liturgy. However, it went no deeper. Like their new theological mentors whom they adored, they too had been deprived of the training that led to the Mystical Prayer, long since relegated to oblivion. Without the practice—and, therefore, without the development of the prayer where human loving is learnt and brought to perfection, as it is suffused and surcharged with the divine—a comparatively new and superficial if picturesque understanding and expression of the faith would have to suffice.

Only a few years after the arrival of this exciting new theology amongst our student body, a new movement set a far wider group of Catholics afire with fervour. It had its modern origins in Pentecostalism and came to the Catholic faithful through Anglicanism in the late 1960s. While their secular friends were swinging in the nightclubs, they were swinging in the churches. This new Charismatic movement could not be ignored, not least because of the exciting, eye-catching phenomena that took place at its meetings. Healing, slaying in the Spirit, speaking in tongues, and other seemingly supernatural phenomena were witnessed by people like me. Nor could this movement be discredited by its questionable theology because, at least amongst the leadership, it was not questionable and was consonant with their claims that it was the work of the Holy Spirit. Indeed, they claimed that this movement engendered a return to the Spirit and to the vibrant and inspiring spirituality that flourished in the early Church.

Both the New Biblical Theology and the Charismatic movement have given and still give much to the Church. But neither individually nor even when harnessed together have they been able to bring about the long-awaited renewal in the Church for which so many of us yearn deep down in our souls. What we called the New Biblical Theology has survived and been integrated into that best genuine theological training courses for both clerical and lay Catholics alike. So, too, the Charismatic Renewal that was so much alive and vibrant in the late 1960s is still with us. Why, then, are we still waiting for the sort of renewal that replicates the deep-lasting, and well-documented rise and spread of Christianity that took the ancient world by surprise two thousand years ago? The jigsaw pieces that will enable us to see this have already been set before us. Let me now begin by putting them together in a way that we can see the whole picture. See it once was so that you can see it again in the present. Then, it can become the blueprint for the renaissance of Christianity that is so long overdue.

CHAPTER 35

From Charismatic to Mystical Prayer

FROM THE BEGINNING OF ITS ARRIVAL into the Catholic Church in the 1960s, its leadership has always insisted that Charismatic Renewal is not new; indeed, it is as old as Christianity itself and can be seen at its inception on the first Pentecost day. Nor can anyone dispute their claims when even such a notable scholar as Monsignor Ronald Knox has studied in particular Charismatic spirituality in the early Church in his book *Enthusiasm*, which was long before the arrival of the Charismatic movement in the Catholic Church.

The three thousand or more converts to Christianity on the first Pentecost and the thousands who would soon follow, inspired by and animated by the Holy Spirit, would at least be indistinguishable from contemporary Charismatics after they were baptised in the Spirit. However, there was a difference, although this might not be immediately apparent. It was not just a racial difference since ninety-nine percent of the first converts were Jews, but it was because they were Jews. It was because they were faithful and devout Jews who had come from all over the Empire to celebrate the anniversary of the day when God had given his law to Moses on Mount Sinai. Therefore, they would have known their Bibles inside out; many would have known it by heart. Furthermore, they knew the inner meaning of God's Word, his promise first made to Abraham,

150

and the further promises made to Prophets, Priests, and Kings. They knew, too, and were waiting for the time when all would be brought to completion. They yearned for the day when their Messiah would come to embody these promises and inaugurate a new world where their God would rule, and where other gods and tyrants had ruled before.

There was another difference that sadly and all too often distinguished them from their modern counterparts. As we have already seen, the first Charismatics had been from birth committed to a daily timetable for prayer that invariably characterised their daily lives, come hell or high water. This commitment did not end with their conversion but was enhanced by it, enabling them to show repeatedly their daily commitment to God in prayer. Furthermore, they sought and continued to seek him, not because of the special graces they seemed to experience, but whether they received them or not. The enthusiasm that inspired them and the psychological buzz were never seen as an end in itself but as a means. It was a means that, when harnessed to a strict daily timetable for prayer, naturally led to Mystical Prayer and to the union with their Messiah, now their Risen Lord, that even the most insightful of their mentors had never envisaged.

However, they were not only endowed with an extraordinary biblical knowledge that would enable them to construct the whole spiritual edifice and fabric of the early Church but with a vital and living faith in the Risen Christ in whom they now lived and moved and had their being. It was natural that they all wanted to know more and in detail about the Messiah whom the first Apostles and the first disciples had come to know and love as Joshua bar Joseph. Those who had known their Messiah in person did not disappoint them. They were not just told story after story about their Saviour but were also taught how to meditate daily on his life, death, and Resurrection. This meditation was naturally enhanced by their biblical knowledge and the realisation, therefore, that the man on whose life they meditated was not just the Messiah but the living God himself into whose life and love they were called to participate. They were taught how to exchange the time they had already allotted to vocal prayer, for meditation time, dwelling on their Saviour's life, death, and Resurrection. Their commitment to daily vocal prayer was then extended to their daily meditation and, therefore, to contemplation, which is its natural consummation. The exciting new enthusiasm for the Good News they had just heard and the inspired fervour they experienced was not a passing fad that would soon fade away.

The truth was that the same Holy Spirit who filled them with his presence showed them that this news fulfilled all they had been waiting for and more. The Messiah had not only come but was both man and God. He had already been raised from the dead and was with them now and to the end of time. The giving of the Old Law to Moses that they had come to celebrate would be superseded by a New Law, the love of God. This New Law was not written on stone tablets to travel with them through the desert in a tent or a tabernacle; it would be written on their hearts with the love they had already seen shining out of St Peter and the first Apostles, just as new converts would soon see this love shining out of them. Once they were baptised, this love would raise them up more and more fully into their new Risen Lord. Then, to the measure that they were sufficiently purified, they would find their new home in him, where in, with, and through him, they would come to love the Father who sent him.

They were of course blessed because they had at hand many saintly men and women, including the Apostles, who had known Christ personally. They would teach the new converts to come to know and love him as he once was, too, so that his love would draw them up into Christ as he is now. This knowing meant that they would never in future be alone and would at all times have access to the love of God through Christ. The initial burst of fervour that enabled them to come to know and love him in their daily meditation soon led them into contemplation. Here, they had the help of others who had gone before them to understand the inner mystical purification that would prepare them for the close and intimate union with their Messiah.

The very essence of the Church, which is not primarily to be seen in buildings made of bricks and mortar but in Christ's new Mystical Body made of men and women filled with his love, was already in place, albeit like a mustard seed. However, as they all began to grow into Christ, they shared in his contemplation of his Father and also in the fruits of this contemplation that would gradually transform them as it had transformed Christ while he was on earth. In this way, their faith would deepen to flower in love, a quality of love pouring out of them that the world had never seen before. These fruits of contemplation developed through love would enable them to convert a pagan world living in darkness into a new Christian world that lived in the light of the Holy Spirit. Over the last fifty years, I have watched with great interest but also much sorrow as I have seen how the Charismatic movement has failed to develop as their first counterparts developed in the early Church. That the Holy Spirit called many people through this movement is quite evident to me, as it would have been quite evident in the early Church, but unlike its predecessors, it has failed to deliver what was being asked of it.

Within fifty years following the Resurrection, most of the Gospels, the Acts of the Apostles, and the Epistles had been written. Christianity was now well established and thriving in almost all the major cities in the Roman Empire. St Peter and St Paul, with very many thousands of others, had been martyred, and Pope Linus 1 ruled over a well-organised and continually growing Church. If you compare the impact of Charismatic Renewal on the modern world in the last fifty years or more to its influence on the ancient pagan world in the same time span, it is immediately evident that something is wrong. In the same period of time, since the Charismatic movement swept into the Church in the late 1960s, I have seen virtually no impact on the wider world outside the Church, where its influence has been negligible. It may well have been a help and inspiration to individuals for a time. Still, unless first enthusiasm is properly supported with appropriate theological teaching and directed by a wise and holy leadership, it will inevitably flounder. That theological and biblical knowledge was immediately available to the first Charismatics, as we have seen. But something else was of vital importance that their modern contemporaries too easily forget. I am referring to the daily time they gave to personal prayer many times daily in the synagogue or in their own homes—a well-ingrained habit born of the Jewish spirituality that formed them.

The first apostles led by example. The moment they received the Holy Spirit, they did not believe they were already prepared and equipped to change the world, so they retired into a prolonged retreat in Jerusalem, as did St Paul elsewhere. He spent ten years preparing to receive the fruits of the contemplation, which he received from his Risen Lord. Christ said that that you will know them by their fruits, and it was by the fruits of the contemplation that they shared with Christ that the unprecedented growth and expansion of the early Church took place. In my experience, large numbers of those caught up in Charismatic Renewal in the late 1960s disappeared from it a decade later. When first fervour evaporated, many drifted away, not just from the Charismatic movement but even from their faith, or at least they became no more than the nominal Christians they had been before. The vapours of emotional euphoria blinded them to the deep spiritual foundations that were in place in the early Church that guaranteed the growth of the first Charismatic Christians into the Church. Although the Charismatic movement may like to point out that at the end of each decade or so, their numbers have remained constant or even increased, it is not because the members from the previous decade have all remained and welcomed new members. It is rather that new members continually come and go without a constant membership being led on to practise the daily prayer and meditation that leads to Mystical Contemplation. It was this contemplation in which their heartbeats began to synchronise with those of Christ that served as the spiritual foundation on which early Christianity was built. Many remained, even though the spiritual feelings that fired them before had frozen over simply because they had no other home to go to or because they felt that their leadership was still important. Sadly, this conviction has not been proven by their ability to lead those in need to travel onward through mystical purification to the union for which they yearn. In fact, they have encouraged many who were ready for true God-given contemplation to accept its man-made counterfeit by generating psychological states of peace and tranquillity by the endless repetition of mantras.

The immediacy with which spiritual euphoria can envelop newcomers can lead to false conclusions. It can lead them to believe that their first fervour is not so much a means to union with God but an end in itself. This misconception can lead to new Charismatics believing that they have arrived at the summit of the spiritual life. The same is true for those who, through personal prayer, experience of first fervour through meditation. A good and early example of this can be seen in the Exercises of St Ignatius when meditation, or more precisely 'Acquired Contemplation' is seen as the high point of the spiritual life because a person is filled with the same sort of spiritual fervour that fires Charismatics. This misconception is exacerbated by calling this meditation *contemplation*, which no previous spiritual writers have ever done. Therefore, once a person experiences first fervour through meditation (or what they mistakenly call *contemplation*), it is believed, contrary to the example of the apostles and the saints who followed them, that it is the time to rush out to change the world through what they call

155

contemplation in action. Then they return again and again to be recharged with spiritual enthusiasm, at least until the well runs dry, as it inevitably does.

That is why you find no teaching at all on the Mystical Theology that is either ignored as unnecessary or attacked as dangerous in official Jesuit spirituality and, for that matter, the spirituality of the modern Charismatic movement. But, thanks to the consequences of Quietism, the same could be said for the other older religious orders who have forgotten their origins, with only a few exceptions, from what was the norm in early Christian Spirituality. Please remember that the essence of Mystical Theology is to teach the selfless, sacrificial loving that can alone open us to God's love. If this does not follow first fervour, then adolescent Christians will never grow up, and we will be condemned to be led, at best, by spiritual striplings and their volatile whims and wishes.

Without receiving the fruits of contemplation which enables them to practise the infused virtues, Christians must act like Stoics and try to practise the moral virtues for themselves, without the grace given in true Mystical Contemplation. Failure is only a matter of time, but until then, woe betide those who would oppose them, for spiritual pride does not countenance opposition. Without receiving the Wisdom that is one of the first fruits of contemplation, they must practise what they call *discernment* instead. It is a man-made system of seeking the truth for non-contemplatives that is fraught with danger because it is practised by human beings blissfully unaware that they are at the mercy of their own unpurified unconscious, or what Freud called the *Id*. In the last fifty years, I have seen this discernment process devastate both individuals and whole communities. But sadly, practitioners are immune to change. Emotional commitment to those who promote modern Christian Humanism is too deeply embedded, preventing them from listening to the God-centred Spirituality introduced into early Christianity by Jesus Christ himself.

If they have the humility to do so, it is not too late for the Charismatic movement to do for the modern Church what they did for the early Church. To do this, they need proper and ongoing theological instruction; they need to realise that they are only at the beginning of the spiritual journey despite experiencing eye-catching phenomena that can lead them to believe otherwise. Finally, they need good spiritual directors who know how to lead them onward into true Mystical Prayer, which was the foundation on which the early Christian Church was founded, and the daily commitment to personal prayer that was mandatory in the early Church.

CHAPTER 36

From Meditation to Contemplation

OVER THE LAST THIRTY YEARS or so, I have sent innumerable articles to newspapers, magazines, and periodicals describing Mystical Contemplation, and I have always found a similar response. In order to depict what I am trying to say, a sub-editor, or whosoever else is given the job of finding something to illustrate what I am trying to say, invariably finds a picture of a monk in a monastery. He is either walking around the cloister with eyes cast down, looking into the middle distance in the garden, or gazing at the tabernacle from the choir stalls. I hope that by now, my readers will know the message that I have been trying to emphasise over and over again in different ways.

The God-given Mystical Spirituality that Jesus Christ introduced into the early Church was first practised by lay people for hundreds of years before monks were even thought of. Like the Jewish spirituality from which it emerged, Christianity began in the home, where it was first learnt and practised by mothers and fathers and brothers and sisters. In those days, what is introduced today in the classroom as catechetics was first introduced in the home through family love inspired by and infused with the Divine Loving of their Risen Lord. Through the sacrament of marriage, it was this loving that daily bonded parents ever more deeply together and that overflowed onto their children. If, like Christ himself or his Apostles, family members sought time outside the home for more intense moments of prayer in solitude, they nevertheless returned to their homes. Here, they would share the fruits of their contemplation before sharing them with the wider world in which they earned their living. But, make no mistake about it, the initial prayer that they were taught, be it different forms of vocal or liturgical prayer or the new form of meditation, would lead to Mystical Contemplation, as can be seen in the experience of St Paul (2 Corinthians 12:1-7).

The only way to God was in, with, and through Christ. Not just in him as an inanimate object but as a loving human being. When Christ contemplates, he is caught up in an act of mutual loving in which his love rises to God, and God's love descends into him. This mutual loving is the Holy Spirit. So, when our prayer life leads us on into Christ and into his contemplation, which it must, else we will never be united with God, something utterly sublime takes place. We are actually led, at least in some measure, into the life of the Three in One, even in this life. This entering is both the ultimate intuition and experience of the great saints and mystics and is the sign of their orthodoxy.

The profound Mystical Spirituality generated and lived in the early Church is not measured by whether or not you find them using the sort of mystical language and terminology that took centuries to find its way into Christian literature. It is measured by the simple principle first enunciated by Christ himself. 'It will be by their fruits that you will know them'. These fruits, detailed by St Thomas Aquinas, which he calls the fruits of contemplation, are freely given to us when our contemplation is one with Christ's own contemplation. For when we are one with him in his contemplation, then we are one with him in our actions in the world that Christ now wants to transform through us.

But contemplation is a God-given gift that cannot be generated by man-made methods or techniques—like mantras that Christ never used himself or taught to his disciples—that charlatans are trying to introduce as true Christian Mystical Prayer today. The Holy Spirit invariably leads a person onward to receive this God-given gift when they have consistently shown their desire to give themselves radically to God by their serious commitment to prayer, not in fits and starts but daily and consistently. I am referring to prayer like meditation for instance, that leads up to and into the Mystic Way. When this happens, contemplative prayer begins quite naturally, for it is the spontaneous, personal, and uniquely individual response to God-given loving, whether it seems to bring darkness, as it does, to begin with, or light when a person is sufficiently purified to experience it. As we will soon see, the simplicity of the spontaneous response to God's loving action does not need to be explained because it comes naturally. However, it does need to be elucidated and encouraged, which is what I propose to do.

What I have called *the great spiritual adventure* begins with the desire for God that rises from the depths of every human being because every human being is made for love. Additionally, every human being is made to love God because we are made in God's image and likeness. This desire is kept alive by the daily pattern of vocal prayer that I have detailed earlier in other books and in my video series on prayer to Contemplation, which you can find on the Essentialist Press website. However, if our desire for God is to be further activated in such a way that it yearns ever more deeply for God, then something further is required. It must be directed to God in such a way that it can come to know and love him ever more deeply and ever more fully. This direction toward God is precisely what happens in meditation. At the high point of meditation, called *Acquired Contemplation* when through meditating on God's love as embodied in Jesus Christ, what was but a subtle and gentle yearning for God now becomes a craving. This craving raises our desire for union with him to such a level that meditating on him as he once was, is replaced by a craving for him as he is now. The truth

160

is that it is only now that we can be united with him, not as he was but as he is now.

That is why I have likened our desire for God to a spaceship. Meditation has acted like the boosters which enable the rocket (symbolising our yearning for God) to rise off the ground and pass through the world's atmosphere. But the gravitational pull would keep it earthbound. Suddenly and alarmingly for the traveller, the boosters must be cast away. The desire to meditate on God's love, as it once manifested itself in Christ in the past, is replaced by a desire to be united with him as he is now in the present. Therefore, the adventure that we have embarked upon enters a new phase. In this new phase, without the competent help of someone who has travelled before us, we think the adventure is over. St John of the Cross said that ninety percent of those who have come so far give up. The reality of the situation is that this is where the adventure begins in earnest. If it were possible to see the whole of the spiritual life as lived by a perfect practitioner on earth in the form of a graph, then meditation would probably take up less than five percent of the whole journey in this life. Meanwhile, contemplation would take up the other ninety-five percent. Let me now turn to contemplation, a gift of God, and what we can best do to facilitate its reception and its practice in our lives.

CHAPTER 37

The Meaning of Contemplation

VOLTAIRE ONCE SAID that God created man in his own image and likeness, and man has returned the compliment. Although first fervour or first enthusiasm has the distinctive benefit of surcharging the desire for God with powerful waves of energy that I have likened to the boosters on a spaceship, they do also have a distinctive downside. The trouble is the receiver is filled with delusions of spiritual grandeur, feeling as I did that I had arrived at the heights of the spiritual life. We can believe that we not only see and experience God as he is in himself but also his plan for humanity and our part in bringing it to the world, beginning with the world around us. In brief, as Voltaire so rightly observed, we can create God in our own image and likeness and then fall in love with him! Travellers, beware, lest it is not by Christ that you are being led, but by a Narcissus instead.

Fortunately, for those who were unlucky enough to share the novitiate with me when I was going through my first fervour, my dyslexia saved them from suffering from the vicissitudes of my newfound 'wisdom'. After all, who would listen to the religious rhapsodies of an imbecile who stammered and stuttered his way through the Latin of the Divine Office? Or the novice who couldn't translate the order's constitutions during the morning classes in the novitiate library and who bumbled and stuttered his way through the spiritual masterpieces that were chosen for reading in the refectory? However, in the wider world and from time immemorial, nominal Christians and even those well advanced in the spiritual life have had to suffer from the emotional and adolescent spiritual pronouncements of those convinced that they have recently been transported into the Transforming Union. Thanks to the sweet vapours of first fervour, they are blind to the unpurified demons within that rule them from what Freud called the *Id*, their deep unconscious mind where powerful and evil drives and impulses determine their behaviour without them even realising it.

Thus, in the next stage of the great spiritual adventure upon which they have embarked, they will, if they persevere, be led into what St John of the Cross calls *The Dark Night of the Soul*. Whether they like it or not, this is where they will be forced to see what their inner demons have been doing for years to prevent them from becoming their true selves that love alone can make of them. Furthermore, they will be made to realise that unless their power is destroyed at source by a power beyond their own, they will continue on the road to spiritual decline. This destruction of self-will is precisely what happens in true contemplative prayer, in which a person is purified for union with God. There is no other way forward than the way of purification at the hands of the Holy Spirit, who led us into the Night for this purpose. Only then can he draw us fully into the life and loving of the glorified Christ to share in the mystery of the Three in One. Spiritual adolescents (and you can be a spiritual adolescent at any age) either persevere to be purified or run away to be continually ruled for the rest of their lives by the demons from within.

In the true Catholic Mystical Contemplation that follows meditation for those who persevere despite the temptations to make a run for it, God does but one thing. He presents himself to the believer not as they would make him in their minds or depict him in their imaginations but as he is in himself. In short and in the words of St John, as 'love', or perhaps more precisely as 'Loving'. That is who he is and what he does all the time. Contemplation can be described as the Contemplation of Light or the Contemplation of Darkness in so far as the receiver experiences it. At the beginning of the Mystic Way, contemplation is always experienced and, therefore, described as the 'Contemplation of Darkness'. That is because God's love initially highlights all the sinfulness and all the evils present in us that prevent the union with himself, which has been his plan for humanity from the outset. That is why, in the first nine or so chapters of his book, *Dark Night of the Soul*, St John of the Cross details what I have called the demons that rule from within the nether regions of our personalities and the sins that they induce us to fall into. Once a person has been sufficiently purified, we begin to experience, in some comparatively small measure, what we will experience without measure in the next life. These experiences are best detailed in St Teresa of Avila's masterpiece, *Interior Castle*.

The 'Contemplation of Darkness' and the 'Contemplation of Light' can be best imagined by likening them to colour. At first, the contemplation of Darkness begins as hardly more than a shade of grey—so subtle that it is hardly detectable, and it gradually deepens to pitch black with every shade of grey in between, but only for those who persevere in this purification. Exactly the same happens with the 'Contemplation of Light' until what appears at first to be a subtle shade of yellow finally becomes true gold, shining with glory. Confusion often muddles students as different mystics often give different names to different shades of black or yellow. Although it may seem logical for the 'Contemplation of Light' to follow once the 'Contemplation of Darkness' has been completed, both come and go throughout the Mystic Way as inseparable and indispensable experiences that characterise mystical purification in this life. That is, at least, until a person arrives at the Mystical Marriage when the Contemplation of Light finds its continual consummation, that not only involves the mind (or what some mystics call the *apex mentis)* but the body, too, that has been transformed and transfigured in the mystical purification.

Throughout his life on earth, right up to his death on the Cross, Christ experienced at all times the Mystical Marriage with his Father. There was no evil in him preventing him from what prevents us from sharing this mystical oneness with his Father. However, he did have to suffer the evil in others when directed against him. Nevertheless, this did not destroy the continual, mutual loving that bonded him to his Father. After his Ascension into heaven, his new physical body (and now also his Mystical Body) continued to contemplate his Father. After meditation, we begin the purification that gradually enables us to share in this, his mutual loving of his Father. We are, in effect, beginning to share in his mutual loving of his Father because we are in him, the New Temple, and, therefore, able to 'con-template' with him in his loving contemplation of his Father. Now, we can see where the word *con–templation* derives, for it means *to gaze upon the glory of God*—in, with, and through the new Temple, which is Christ. Unlike Christ's contemplation, however, we are very frequently distracted from our purpose by a hundred and one distractions and temptations that arise from our fallen nature.

Whereas distractions never disturbed Christ, they will continue to disturb us in our 'Dark Night of the Soul' until we are so purified that we can enter in, with, and through him into the Mystical Marriage. This purification can be brought about only after very many years, or rather decades, in which the arrogance that once possessed the spiritual adolescent is replaced by humility. This humility alone that can enable us to contemplate the Father without any let or hindrance, in, with, and through the New Temple, which is Christ. Only then will we be able to 'see God'—not as Voltaire says, as we have created him in our own image and likeness. Rather, we will see him as he is in himself.

CHAPTER 38

A Subtle Presence

IN THE CATHOLIC TRADITION, Mystical Contemplation is a pure gift of God that we cannot attain by our own efforts alone. If, therefore, you are ever offered instant forms of self-generated contemplation from Indian 'mystics' from the East or their Catholic mimics in the West, you are being offered the counterfeit. True Catholic contemplation comes after the meditation that naturally leads into it. By *meditation*, I do not mean the repetitions of mantras that the apostles never taught but the meditation that they did teach—the daily, prayerful reflection on the most lovable man to have ever lived on this earth, who embodies within himself the infinite love of God. This meditation gradually surcharges our desire for God, who is our final destiny. It is then, in the contemplation into which the Holy Spirit now leads us, our contemplation is joined with Our Risen Lord's contemplation. In him, our desire for God is purified, enabling us to receive his love that contains all our needs in this world and in the next.

However, everything depends on our desire, our will, our love, which in contemplation, must be purified of all else that would turn it away from God. To the measure that this is done will be the measure in which our love will then be united with Christ's love, to become a two-way current, enabling our love to rise to God and his love to descend into us. This exchange enables us to receive the fruits of contemplation, without which we can do very little for God or for others. Christ himself made it quite clear at the Last Supper that without him, we have no power to do anything (John 15:1-6). However, contemplation will grow and develop only to the degree in which we respond to the loving action of the Holy Spirit, who is the mutual loving that unites the Father to the Son.

When St Peter was asked how to respond to the Holy Spirit on the first Pentecost, he said we must repent. In modern English, St Peter was saying that we must keep turning from that which is not of God and opening ourselves to receive God in the fullness of who He is. If we continually persevere in doing this, then the Holy Spirit will do the rest, and the whole of the Mystic Way will unfold before us. To do this, observe the principle that, as I have already said, I discovered while in the Novitiate from a book on Mystical Prayer, which I found in the library. I repeat it once more, for it is so important: 'When sweet meditation leads you into dark contemplation be sure that you give to your new prayer exactly the same time as you gave to the preceding prayer'. This continual self-sacrifice is not just a prayer in itself; it is the most important prayer we can ever make because it unites us to Christ's sacrificial prayer that he made continually while he was on earth. In the adventure that is now beginning, we will see how, through our selfless acts of prayer, we are uniting our life to his life as we practise the same sort of self-sacrifices that he made for us.

This brings us to what we must do to be ready and open to receive the fruits of contemplation when our contemplation is united with Christ's contemplation. In short, we must continually make spontaneous acts of prayer that will eventually become a continual habit of prayer or a continual habit of selfless giving or offering, uniting us with the ongoing self-sacrificial loving that characterised Christ's life. Ultimately, this will lead to an abiding disposition of heart and mind, enabling a person to abide in God and God to abide in them at all times, as he did in Jesus Christ when he was on earth. What St Angela of Foligno calls 'The School of Divine Love' begins in earnest when we are led into contemplation and are asked to continually try to keep on loving God when he seems to have left us and left us permanently. I cannot tell you how to respond to God at the beginning of what is called *Dark Contemplation* because the prayer must come from the very depth of *your* own being. As St Paul insists, the Holy Spirit will prompt you because what is now beginning is his work, the work of your redemption, your transformation, and your final transfiguration through love (Romans 8:26–27).

His love is so strong that, at first, it seems to be doing nothing because it is like an irresistible force striking the immovable object of our own all-enveloping sinfulness that rises from the Original Sin ruling us from within. Therefore, nothing seems to be happening. Nor will anything happen until we sufficiently persevere in true, selfless loving. I mean the loving that is learnt in what is sometimes called *Obscure Contemplation*. When we continually and persistently try to go on giving and go on loving when we seem to receive nothing in return, our desire to be united with God is purified, sharpened, and ever more finely honed through the purification to which we have freely submitted ourselves. In this persistence, we relentlessly practise the selfless, unalloyed, and unconditional loving that can alone unite us to the love of God. Although nothing seems to be happening sometimes for very many months, a deep interaction of mystical mutual loving is making our heart's desire ever more sensitive, docile, pliant, and eventually porous to the Holy Spirit. This docility enables the believer to receive what is perhaps the first gift of God that he gives us through his Holy Spirit. This first gift is to realise deep down within us that despite all evidence to the contrary, God is in this strange new world that we have been drawn into, despite the endless temptations to cut and run. Somehow, what is called the *sensus fidelium* is awakened within us. This *sensus fidelium* is an intuitive sense for orthodoxy that the

Holy Spirit infuses into those who earnestly seek him in the prayer beyond first beginnings.

Furthermore, we experience something, perhaps for the first time, that we will realise with ever greater conviction as our journey continues. We receive the gift of wisdom to see what we should do, and we are simultaneously given the grace to put what we know we should do into practice. Even before we experience that tenuous sense of presence to which I have already referred, we begin to realise that, although we seem to be receiving nothing that could be described as tangible from God, we are, in fact, receiving the first gift of the Holy Spirit. This gift is the gradual but certain realisation that without this strange new form of prayer that nobody seems to understand, least of all ourselves, we somehow feel morally and spiritually depleted without it.

Gradually, this subtle presence begins to grow until, eventually, we know, without doubt and without anyone else telling us, that we are indeed on the way. We are on the way to the destiny for which we have been created in the first place. But be sure of this: in the lifelong mystical roller coaster upon which we have embarked, more time will be spent in 'downs' rather than in 'ups' in the journey ahead. For the truth of the matter is that the thoroughly selfish and sinful traveller must be prepared and purified to be united with the most perfect man who ever lived so that their prayer and his prayer can be as one. Then we will be able to receive from the Father, to whom we pray, the only wisdom that is worth having because it comes not from man but from God.

CHAPTER 39

The Most Powerful Prayer of ALL

MY DOCTOR HAS ALWAYS BELIEVED that the Irish are, in fact, one of the lost tribes of Israel. I initially took his conviction with a pinch of salt; that is until I began to study Aramaic, when I had to think again. Let me explain what I mean.

When the ancient Jews gave a person a name, that name was meant to define their identity and their purpose—who they were and what they did. Thus, when God finally told his people his name, he told them that it is Love. When St John said that God is Love, he was only repeating what Jesus himself had told him and the other Apostles. That is what he is in himself, as well as what he does. Notice that this name was not a noun but a verb, so God was both Love and Loving simultaneously. We do not have a tense in the English language to help us appreciate precisely what this means; however, the 'present continuing tense' in the Irish language does. It means that God has loved us, is loving us, and will continue to love us forever.

To explain this to us, God sent us his only Son, who was, and still is, the flesh-and-blood embodiment of his infinite loving. Consequently, all who were, and still are, open to receiving his Son's love will receive the self-same life and love that animates him now. This love can save us all from enthralment to the selfishness and sinfulness that is the cancer of the soul. Therefore, God insisted that his Son be called Jesus, which means *the One who saves us, the deliverer,* or *the Saviour*—because only his love can do what nothing else can do. That it is why his holy name is the most powerful name on earth, as St Paul tells us (Philippians 2:10-11). It should not be surprising then that it was made into and constantly used as a prayer in the early Church that came to be called *The Jesus Prayer*. Repeating this prayer in its shortest form, as taught by Abbot Macarius, became a special act of devotion. Additionally, it was particularly championed by St Bernard and then by the Dominican and Franciscan schools of spirituality.

However, it was with St Bernadine of Siena (1380-1444) and his fellow Franciscan reformers of the fifteenth century that this devotional practice took off in a major way. He told the hundreds of thousands of his followers to enshrine the word Jesus on their hearts and continually recite it with their tongues, but, lest they forget to do this, to do something else as well. The abbreviation for the Greek word for Jesus, IHS (Ihsous), was used by ancient scribes. For St Bernadine, it became a monogram, or Christogram, that he encouraged them to place in and outside their churches, public buildings and inside and outside their own homes, as tourists can still see all over Italy to this day. The genius of this short prayer is that it can be just as helpful to beginners on their spiritual journey as it can be to those advanced in the Mystic Way. Remember the advice of Abbot Isaac to John Cassian to use the prayer 'O God come to my aid, O Lord make haste to help me' throughout the day to keep the mind and heart fixed on God.

You can do the same with the simple prayer 'Jesus', as my mother did. It is particularly helpful when the spiritual life deepens, for then the simpler the prayer, the better. What better prayer to make than this: calling on his name for help in good times and in hard times when all seems to be well or when everything seems to be falling apart? Then, when mystical purification is at its height and only a single word is as much as a person can muster, what more appropriate word can be used as a prayer for spiritual succour and support than using the Holy Name of Jesus? When, towards the end of her life, my mother was lying in bed, seriously ill, with her rosary beads in her hand, she was almost in tears. She told me she could no longer say her favourite prayer as she used to. All she could say was the single word, the simplest and most powerful of all prayers: the holy name of Jesus. When, after her death, I told my father about her tears, he said they were not tears of pain but of joy. He said she had been more joyful at the end of her life than at any other time.

After the Renaissance and the decline of the Greek language in favour of Latin, the IHS came to be used as an acronym for the Latin, *'Jesus Hominum Salvator'*, meaning 'Jesus Saviour of Humankind'. The three nails used to fix Jesus to the Cross were then added to the monogram, and a small cross was mounted on the letter 'H'. There is no letter 'J' in the Greek alphabet; therefore, the letter 'I'(iota) was used to write the first letter of the holy name, and that usually remained after the Latin came to be used in the new acronym.

However, lest we should forget, our redemption was not fulfilled with his death on the Cross but with his Glorification, so the monogram was set in a circle of fire. The circle of fire represents the Sun, which, from the earliest times, was seen as a symbol of the Resurrection and Glorification of Jesus. The flames radiating from the perimeter are meant to be a continual reminder of the unquenchable fire of love that Jesus first released upon us all on the first Pentecost day and on every subsequent day for those who are open to receiving it.

When you recite the word 'Jesus' as the prayer *par excellence,* you need say no more. The One who hears your prayer hears your deepest needs that Jesus came to satisfy, even though you may not realise what they are yourself and so cannot find words to express them. When you are in trouble, and the whole world seems to have conspired against you, do not think you must explain your plight to the One who knows anyway; just say the 'Jesus Prayer'. When you are in the blackest moment of the 'Dark Night of the Soul', and the very gates of hell seem to be open to engulf you, just say the 'Jesus Prayer'. It is not a mantra, but the most powerful prayer of all and a prayer which will always be answered because, as Jesus promised at the Last Supper, anything you ask of God in his name will be granted (John 16:23-24). When I asked a contemporary contemplative how he prayed, he said, 'I use the Holy Name followed by the words of St Thomas, *My Lord and My God* and then the prayer of St Francis, *My God and My All,* which is the motto of the Franciscan order. But the prayer I use most is the Holy Name, until Love's response is savoured in Silence'.

If you persevere, come what may, this prayer will gradually lead you into the prayer of experience, when what was asked for in darkness will be received in light. This light is the same love that raised Jesus from the dead and will raise us from the dead, too—from the tomb we have made for ourselves through sin and selfishness. This will enable us to rise in, with, and through Jesus, drawing us up and into his all-engrossing and totally enthralling loving of God. It is here that we are filled with the fruits of this contemplation so that Jesus can continue to do again through us what he first did himself whilst he was on earth and did again through the Apostles and those who followed him after his Resurrection.

CHAPTER 40

The Sacred Heart

THE GREAT CLASSICAL LANGUAGES like Greek and Latin were honed to perfection by philosophers, academics and intellectuals. So, naturally, they were best adapted to emphasising the importance of the mind and intellectual understanding and conveying the conclusions of rational thought. However, when these languages integrated with the vernacular languages of the new inhabitants of Europe, what came to be called the Romance languages rose to become the spoken and written language of the majority. As their names suggest, and because they rise from the experience of ordinary people, they emphasised not so much the intellect or the mind but the feelings and the heart.

So, when nearly three centuries after the great Franciscan reforms of the fifteenth century, there was a need for another Catholic renewal; it was not an intellectual symbol that took pride of place, but the symbol of a human heart. This symbol was not merely any human heart but the heart of Jesus Christ himself, as revealed to St Margaret Mary. This love had no other purpose than to overflow onto others to fill their hearts, too, and those who look to them for spiritual fulfilment. This revelation was quite timely because it came when, outside the Church, the Enlightenment was overemphasising the mind at the expense of the heart. This intellectual movement was focusing on something else, too. Inside the Church, the new emphasis on moralism at the expense of mysticism (thanks to the heresy of Quietism) was imbued with Jansenism, which has infected the Church up to modern times (supposing 'modern times' includes the times when I grew up in the middle of the last century!). Jansenism is a sort of Catholic Calvinism promoting a strict moral code, often enforced with myriad moral rules and regulations. It resembled what happened to the Judaism into which Christ was born, in which the devout Jew would have to observe to the letter over 600 rules and regulations almost daily to deem himself pleasing to the God of love whom they had latterly re-created as a sort of supernatural punctilious policeman. The new religion of love that was rejected by his own but accepted by the new people of God in the early Church, was being offered once more through the devotion to the Sacred Heart of Jesus, which arose and expanded in the eighteenth, nineteenth, and twentieth centuries.

The rise of the New Biblical Theology emphasised a communal liturgical spirituality that tended to downplay the personal piety in which many had grown up. Theological snobs like me, who were taken up with the Paschal Mystery and the liturgy surrounding it, tended to forget that at the heart of that mystery was the heart of Christ, which was continually loving God and drawing all who were open to him into that profound mystical loving. No matter how this liturgy was reformed to represent the ancient liturgy, it would become the power that it used to be only to the measure in which it represented the daily sacrificial loving of the faithful who took part in it. By this I mean the daily sacrificial acts through prayer and good works that would enable their offerings to be united with Christ, their Risen Lord. Their Risen Lord is no other than Christ in the act of Loving God his Father. This continual, dynamic, divine loving is what Christ himself asked St Margaret Mary to call his Sacred Heart. For, then and now, it was the best way to present the central mystery of our faith to those whose faith had been reduced to rules and regulations by Catholic Calvinists who had lost their way.

Among Jesus' last words recorded in Saint John's Gospel are 'Blessed are those who have not seen and yet believe' (John 20:29). Throughout the subsequent centuries, Christian art has tried to help those of us 'who have not seen' to come to know and love not just the Christ who lived in history, but the Christ who still lives in Majesty. As memories grew dimmer, Christian art became more and more important, particularly for those who were illiterate. The representation of Christ that dominated the first great Basilicas was of Christ in Majesty, the *Pantocrator*, the ruler of all, that so many like to place as small icons on the walls of their homes today.

This image tended to make Christ appear somewhat distant until, in the wake of the crusades, the Holy Land was opened to the West, and a new spirituality began to flourish, thanks to Saint Bernard and Saint Francis, which again emphasised the humanity of Christ. Their influence can be seen in painters like Giotto and the great Renaissance artists. However, thanks to Saint Margaret Mary, a new popular art began to represent not just Christ as he was but as he is now, with a glorified body bursting with uncreated love for us. The Sacred Heart is the same as the Pantocrator, but now he does not appear as distant, for he rules with all the human love that filled Jesus while he was on earth but transformed by his glorification in heaven.

Devotion to the Sacred Heart has at times been trivialised by bad taste in the cult surrounding it and the art used to promote it. Nevertheless, it should never be forgotten, as it proclaims a profound truth that is the central truth of our faith. Jesus is not dead, but he has risen and is alive now, bursting with uncreated life and love pouring out of his heart relentlessly and into the hearts of all who would receive him. For two centuries, this devotion counteracted 'Catholic Calvinism' or Jansenism with its narrow-minded, kill-joy moralism by proclaiming the love of the Risen Christ in a way that even the simplest could understand. No one should allow their artistic sensibilities to prevent them from appreciating this profound truth that was revealed in a unique way to Saint Margaret Mary. The Sacred Heart is not just incarnate love but incarnate loving, who will transform all who open their hearts to receive his love and then draw their loving into his loving.

When I was a boy, only two devotions would fill churches during the week. They were devotions to St Anthony and devotions to the Sacred Heart. Devotions to the Sacred Heart armed ordinary Catholics with a plethora of short prayers like 'Sacred Heart of Jesus, I put my trust in thee', which my mother taught me amongst many others that help the faithful to centre their daily spiritual lives on their Risen Lord whose picture was set in pride of place in their homes, as it was in my home.

Thanks to photography (what I call a modern miracle), contemporary artists are able to paint perhaps the most accurate likeness of Christ ever seen. From the image of the Shroud, artists have recreated Christ's face after his death on the Cross. A copy of this painting hangs on my bedroom wall, reminding me in a most moving way of the Sacred Heart of Jesus, who gave his all for us and who invites us to give our all for him in return.

CHAPTER 41

Devotion to the Passion of Christ

A FOREBEAR OF MINE, a Catholic priest called Richard Tork-ington, was made the Rector of the local Parish by the Lord of the Manor, a man called Thomas Boleyn, who had a famous daughter called Ann! But Richard will be known for something more important than that, for he made a diary of his pilgrimage to the Holy Land just before the Protestant Reformation began in 1517. Henceforth, he would have a special devotion to the Passion of Christ. St Francis of Assisi also went on pilgrimage to the Holy Land. He was particularly devoted to the Passion of Christ so that his subsequent blindness was put down to the endless weeping for what the man he called Brother Jesus endured for our salvation. His illustrious son, St Bonaventure, who was perhaps the greatest spiritual writer of the thirteenth century, implored his readers to dwell continually on the Passion and death of Christ in prayer. It is not surprising then that the Stations of the Cross are still celebrated daily in Jerusalem by the Franciscan guardians of the Holy Land. However, this profound devotion is not the special prerogative of a particular religious order but of the whole Catholic Church.

It would be a mistake to relegate this deeply moving devotion to Lent alone, as it can take us to the heart and soul of Christ's love for us as we gaze at fourteen terrible moments in his life when he gave his all for us. If it is not possible to do this in church,

178

then do it at home either by physically moving from one station to another or by poring over the different scriptural accounts of Christ's Passion and death. Imagine that you are there, gazing at the person who loves you more deeply than any other. Then, you will begin to pray, not in long sentences, but in short, pithy phrases as the situation demands. I will not give examples from my own or others' prayers because these expressions of love are so deeply and uniquely personal that privacy forbids it. I have, however, always used the prayer that our Parish priest prayed at the end of each station because what it expressed coincided with my own feelings: 'I love you Jesus, my love, above all things. I repent with my whole heart for having offended you; never permit me to be separated from you again, grant that I may love you always, then do with me what you will'.

In practising the Stations of the Cross or meditating on Christ's Passion and death, we automatically find that our expressions of love and devotion become shorter and shorter, almost in direct proportion to the power of the feelings and emotions that rise up from within us. As in all loving words, they give way to a deep contemplative stillness when the full reality of love, or rather of being loved, begins to take hold. Christ's love for us does the same, gradually becoming ever more engrossing, ever more enthralling, and ultimately life changing. If we make this love the ongoing love of our life, it will lead us to the fullness of love, or the infinite love that God has prepared for us as our final destiny. How can infinite love be expressed in human words and actions? In short, it cannot. But the love we see expressed in the Stations of the Cross as Christ stutters and staggers in pain and agony to the place of his final humiliating death on the Cross is as close as human words and actions can come to it. Just as I have described before in this spiritual journey, the love generated in meditation must be purified before we can not only express our love for Christ in human emotions and feelings but also be united with him now in his Risen Glory. Therefore, both the love that is identified with the will as well as the love that is felt in our human emotions must be purified.

Common sense should tell us that a deep purification must occur before we can be united with God's love as embodied in Jesus Christ. If this purification is completed in this life, as in many of the lives of the saints, then purgatory in the next will be superfluous. Contrary to the belief of the ancient Gnostics and Neoplatonists and their 'Catholic' descendants today, preparation for union with God includes the whole of our human personality. In other words, it does not just mean the purification of our spiritual selves, of our love, or our wills, but our bodies, too, together with the human feelings and emotions through which we express our love. The One with whom we are to be united still has a body, albeit a mystical body, but a body, nevertheless, that has been transformed and transfigured by glory. That is why our bodies must be purified together with our human feelings and emotions. During the purification, these human emotions are dormant but not dead. After purification, they are reawakened and brought back to life, free of the evil inclinations that originally disfigured them. This reawakening enables us to be united with Christ like never before.

This profound union finds its completion in this life in what the great mystics call the Mystical Marriage or the transforming union. That is why St Francis of Assisi's tears were even more abundant after his purification than before. Because then, his human response to the sufferings of Brother Jesus was far more profoundly human than before, when having been purified, they returned to him, freed from anything that could sully their purity. That is why they were more vibrant, more expressive, and more active than ever before. This new realness impelled him to pray to share in Christ's sufferings, and God granted him the privilege of receiving the stigmata to do so. But he also prayed to experience the love that impelled Christ to give his all for us, too. This prayer was also granted and was to be seen in moments of ecstatic bliss and otherworldly joy that endeared him to all. They saw in him what they aspired to become—the complete human being that inspired the medieval world to call St Francis 'The Second Christ'. Purification must include not just our hearts and minds but our bodies, too, including our human feelings and emotions, because it is only in this way that we can experience the love of God in, with, and through the physical but glorified body of Jesus Christ in this world and in the next and to all eternity. The mystery of the Transfiguration not only shows what would become of Christ and his human body after his Resurrection but what will happen to ours too when united with his.

CHAPTER 42

Cognitive Therapy and the Seven Deadly Sins

THE BEST, THE MOST CERTAIN, and the most permanent way of putting out fire is by depriving it of oxygen. What is true of physical fire is also true of spiritual fire. Long before Freud turned it into a science, mystics knew that human beings are dominated from within by the fire of deeply embedded passions. These passions rule from the nether regions of our personalities without us even realising it. These mystics were the first to realise that unless these fires were first suffocated and then destroyed at source by love, they had the power to destroy a person both spiritually and physically. Love and love alone—more specifically, God's love—can deprive the passions of the oxygen that enflames them and then unearth and incinerate the evil roots from which they arise.

Prayer is the practical process first taught to believers to harness their human love so that it can be inspired by and infused with divine love and gradually be possessed by that love. This divine love is the only spiritual oxygen that can alone destroy the fires of interior passions. These passions have been traditionally characterised as pride, greed, lust, wrath, gluttony, envy, and sloth and have come to be known as the seven deadly sins. They lurk deep down in the unconscious like evil demons, ready to leap out from their lair to pour oil on the flames of the passions they have ignited in the minds and hearts of the unwary. Here, if they are dwelt upon, they can possess those hearts and minds with their malice before inducing them to act out what they have so far only visualised to the serious harm of others.

As these evil passions manifest themselves in their victims' minds and hearts, they must first be confronted here. However, they should not be confronted in a head-to-head collision, which will always be lost, but by subtly generating the love in prayer that will simply suffocate them by depriving their needed oxygen. As the spiritual life progresses, those who persevere will find that the prayer which began at the boundaries of their lives begins to take over from the centre of their lives, overflowing to possess their whole being.

Be sure of this: the evil that is rampant within all of us, whether we are aware of it or not at the beginning, can be destroyed only by the power and quality of divine love that takes years to generate in prayer. That is why prayer must begin immediately, as it did for the first Christians who, as we have seen, spent two years in prayer and fasting even before Baptism. For Christ himself said that only prayer can ultimately do what nothing else can (Mark 9:29). It was to Christ and to the spirituality that he first taught, before it was introduced as the spiritual substratum and foundation of the early Church, that I first turned for inspiration for 'the one thing necessary'.

Just as Jesus said the famous Jewish prayer, the 'Shema' in which all he said and did was offered to God at least three times a day, the first Christians did likewise and, in time, it evolved into what we today call the Morning Offering. Christ himself did not need to meditate in order to contemplate the Father, whose love he had experienced from all eternity, but his followers did. In this meditation, they were taught how to reflect, ruminate, and then contemplate the same love of God that inspired Jesus, but as embodied in his flesh and blood whilst he was on earth. The continual turning away from the evils that tried to prevent them from doing this are effectively continual acts of repentance. Indeed, these acts that say no to self and yes to God generate a quality of selfless loving that enables God's love to enter into them. St Francis put it so simply: it is in giving that we receive. Then, this love further enables us to meditate on and subsequently contemplate God's love as it finds its fullest human expression in Christ's pure, unadulterated goodness, made manifest in all he said and did. It generated for the first time what later, and in modern times, came to be called Cognitive Therapy.

Not everyone has the time or the money to spend years in therapy attempting to overcome, or at least to come to terms with, their demons. But Cognitive Therapy can do the same, certainly more quickly and often more effectively, and patients can be taught to practise it for themselves. Although this therapy was not explicitly taught to early Christians, it was, in fact, practised without them realising it, having both a spiritual and a dramatic psychological effect on their fallen human personalities. However, the essence of Cognitive Therapy was first explicitly realised by one of the great Desert Fathers—Evagrius Ponticus. This practice involved replacing evil or destructive thoughts with good and creative thoughts. What better way of doing this, he realised, than by filling one's mind and heart with thoughts of the highest and most perfect form of love as embodied in the pure, unadulterated goodness of Jesus Christ? Then, in, with, and through him, contemplating this love as manifested in the glory of God himself. When, as we have seen, this love seeps out of set forms of prayer to irrigate the rest of our lives in the contemplation that is transformed into the 'prayer without ceasing', Christian cognitive therapy reaches perfection. In short, the evil thoughts and desires that have been tantalizing our minds and hearts are deprived of the malignant powers of evil that have been feeding them. That is not all; the more we keep turning to receive God's love in prayer, then the more our purified hearts become the prisms that enable that love to shaft down into the nether regions of our fallen human nature to destroy at source the home, the Hades, the Hell from which the demons within rise to enthral us.

Thus, the great Icon of Christ descending into Hell resonated with believers travelling along the Mystic Way, for it filled them with confidence that the One who was purifying them from within was none other than their Risen Lord himself. Furthermore, when his love had completed its work within them, then they would become fully complete and restored human beings transformed into the image and likeness of the most perfect, mature, loving, and complete human being who has ever walked on the face of this earth.

Man-made Cognitive Therapy may restore us to the normal human beings that we were before, but true Christian cognitive therapy goes further. It destroys the evil at source in our unconscious that prevents us from being refashioned into other Christs through whom our Risen Lord chooses to work for the redemption and salvation of all mankind. In short, prayer truly understood and practised daily is where saints are made.

CHAPTER 43

The Inner Dynamics of Prayer

I AM NOT A PARTICULAR FAN of the endless definitions and divisions I had to learn *ad nauseam* for my theology exams, but I must admit that they can often be helpful to clarify something that can otherwise remain obscure. So, let me give you a definition of prayer and then divide it by two! Prayer is *the turning and opening of the mind and heart to God.* Prayer can be divided into 'perfect prayer' and 'imperfect prayer'. Perfect prayer can be seen only in this life as practised by Our Lord Jesus Christ and also (thanks to her Immaculate Conception) by Mary, his mother. They were, at all times, able to turn their minds and hearts to God. Imperfect prayer can be seen as it is practised by everyone else and can be defined as *trying* to turn and open the mind and heart to God.

The operative word Is *trying* because, even with the best will in the world, everybody will find that, short of a direct intervention by God, we will always have distractions and temptations in prayer. In fact, the very essence of prayer for us consists in endlessly trying to turn away from these distractions and temptations. From the very first prayer we are taught, through whatever form of meditation or devotional practice to which we turn and onward into Mystical Prayer, these spiritual gadflies will pester us. Far from destroying our prayer, they can be the means of perfecting it by enabling the person seeking God to generate the quality of self-sacrificial giving that will always induce God to give us what he created us for in the first place. Namely, the love for which we crave more than anything else. Although what we only see as spiritual pests that which seems to beleaguer us the moment we try to pray, they afflict us more intensely than ever before when, after first fervour, we are led into Mystical Prayer.

Remember, the word *mystical* merely means *invisible, unseen or hidden*. So far, although our prayer may be unseen to others, it is clearly visible to us in our minds, our imaginations, and our hearts, but Mystical Prayer is not, hence the name *mystical*. Therefore, it is such a problem for those, and that is the vast majority, who have never been told about mystical purification that is a necessity for all, never mind how to pray in it. It is not just Protestants who deny purgatory, but also Catholics who seem to think we can be united with God without being purified. They may believe in it in the next life, but they do not want to have anything to do with it in this life. They seem to think that they have never had it so good materially, so they might as well enjoy what they have and worry about will come later. Thus, the great Saints and mystics who once led us in the past are so rarely seen amongst us.

I have already explained the historical reasons why Mystical Prayer was removed from the education of priests and religious. And why, therefore, at best, the laity have found little authoritative help or encouragement in the Mystical Prayer life they have been trying to pursue alone. At worst, they have been told they are following a fruitless, if not dangerous, pathway. Presently, spiritual ignoramuses at the very top of our beloved Church, who have forgotten their origins, are specifically trying to dismantle any institution that encourages the Mystic Way and the contemplative form of life promoting it. New Goths are at the Gates of Rome! So, let me emphasise yet again that the God-given spirituality that Christ introduced into the early Church was totally based on love—not primarily our love but God's love. However, this love, like all love, can be received only by those who learn how to receive it, which is by learning how to love. This learning process that I have been trying to explain and encourage reaches its climax in the Mystical Prayer, which has been long forgotten and treacherously attacked by those who have lost their own spiritual way. I encourage those who, thus far, have received but little encouragement by explaining the essence of the process in which human love is practised in such a way that it can be open to receive the divine.

The emotional enthusiasms that first encourage beginners, far from being unimportant, are essential to inspire beginners. They are like reservoirs from which spiritual travellers must drink deeply to sustain them when God leads them into the spiritual desert where genuine love, not cupboard love, is learnt. Giving again and again, even when all that sustained them emotionally before is taken away, is the only way that true selfless, sacrificial loving, which is the heart and soul of our faith, can be learnt. This persistence is the most profound and effective way in which we can take up our daily cross to follow Christ so as to be purified to enter into him as fully as he would wish. As selfless loving is being learnt, most especially when all seems to be spiritually dark and gloomy, we are demonstrating to God the true quality of our selfless loving, to which he will always respond. This demonstration is the very essence of the new worship in spirit and in truth promised by Christ to the Samaritan woman and practised throughout his own life before he bequeathed it to the early Church. A brief *résumé* of how to pray in this, the most testing time in the spiritual life, can best be summed up by referring you to a very great English mystic who wrote *The Cloud of Unknowing* in the middle of the fourteenth century.

When it seems and feels, at the beginning of the Mystic Way, that there is a Cloud of Unknowing between you and God, the author insists that you must place all the distractions and temptations that have followed you into prayer into what he calls a Cloud of For-getfulness beneath you. Then, choose a short prayer that sums up your desire for union with God and repeat it slowly and prayerfully so that you can, at all times, keep what he calls 'your naked intent upon God'. This prayer will eventually, not in weeks but rather in months, enable you to pierce the Cloud, eventually making a mystical passageway through which your love rises to God and his love descends into you. The measure of God's love pouring into you will be determined by the measure of the ongoing selfless lov-ing you have demonstrated in what seems to be, at least at first, a desert without any oases. 'The Prayer of Naked Faith', made by a Christian mystic, finally leads to being drawn up and out of one-self into God's love, experienced to various degrees of intensity. It begins with the Prayer of Quiet, rises to Full Union and then from Ecstasy and the Spiritual Betrothals to the Mystical Marriage, or the Transforming Union, as described by St Teresa of Avila in her masterwork *Interior Castle*. And this is only the prelude to what is to come!

CHAPTER 44

Wisdom from The Curé D'Ars

ALTHOUGH BISHOP PARKER WAS CONSECRATED a Bishop in 1941, it took him almost ten years before he visited his old school. Although we looked forward to seeing him, what excited us more was what he was to bring with him. But let me start the story at the beginning. When she was still a young woman, his mother visited the Curé d'Ars in France to see the parish priest who was the talk of Europe, as stories of his sanctity had spread everywhere. After going to him for confession, the old priest gave her a wooden cross that she was to keep for her son to wear after he was made a Bishop. She had not even thought of being married, so she was astonished to think that she would be the mother of a Bishop.

After his visit, we pestered our former master to read us the story of this prodigious saint. It was full of wonderful stories, some told by the Curé himself, others about him that I have never forgotten. One of the stories tells of a young man who spent many hours bemoaning his sins in his local church. One day, when, as usual, he was engaged in his detailed examination of conscience, dripping with remorse, someone tapped him on the shoulder. Turning around, he discovered that it was Christ. 'Can you not spend more time thinking of me and my love for you,' he asked, 'instead of endlessly pouring over your own misery?' The prevailing self-centred spirituality at the time still emphasised the 'do it yourself spir-

190

ituality' that arose after the Renaissance. It was still emphasised in our school in which a classical education took precedence over any other. It was reinforced by Jesuit retreat masters who instilled into us that the spiritual life begins with, in the words of the Delphic Oracle, 'knowing oneself'.

For this purpose, extensive, twice-daily examinations of conscience would be paramount. Like the classical heroes of antiquity, this would enable us to first know ourselves and then root out the sins that would prevent us from generating for ourselves the virtues with which we wished to be endowed. Rather than putting us off, as teenagers, we were spurred on by this way of achieving our own perfection that primarily depended on our own endeavours. Of course, God's grace was not denied, but the main emphasis we all wanted to hear anyway was of man's power, not God's power.

However, this story and others about the Curé and his simple teaching were enough to alert me and to draw my attention away from the anthropocentric spirituality we were taught to the Gospels' true God-given and God-centred spirituality. In this God-given spirituality, first lived and then taught by Christ, the first Christians were taught how to seek and find God's love in Christ himself, who is continually pouring his love out on all who wish to receive it. It would be available to all persons throughout subsequent centuries and to the end of time. As in all love, when it is first received, it highlights our unworthiness and the sins that prevent us from receiving it. But, most particularly, if it is God's love, it invariably and simultaneously gives us the grace to overcome them.

The second story that comes to mind is of an old man, known for his holiness, who came to church every day to pray for hours on end. When the Curé asked him how he spent his time in these prolonged periods of prayer, he answered simply, 'He looks at me, and I look at him'. This gaze between Creator and creature is perhaps the simplest way that contemplation has ever been explained. That is why this story is told over and over again by those who aspire to practise it. But notice that out of humility, the Curé uses another person to show how contemplation is the source of his own holiness and the holiness of all who practise the contemplation that opens them to receive the fruits of that contemplation. It is to show in his way that this man's renowned holiness was the consequence of the profound contemplative prayer that had filled him with the love that he was contemplating and with all the supernatural gifts and infused virtues.

When the Curé was asked what he found most difficult to face in the spiritual life, he answered without hesitation, 'depression'. No one is depressed when first filled with the emotional joy generated at the beginning of the spiritual life or with the God-given contemplation that fills a person with such deep happiness at the end of it. The depression to which he refers is the depression that comes from seeing rising from within, the personal selfishness and the sinfulness that prevents us from the simple, loving gaze upon the God experienced by St Paul after his personal purification. This was the purification that the Curé had to undergo before he became the saint who drew over forty thousand people a week to see him, to confess to him, to seek his advice, and to hear him speak. The full name of the Curé is not without its significance. He was baptised Jean-Baptiste, and his surname was Vianney. Like his namesake, St John the Baptist, he spent very many years in solitary prayer before the goodness of God finally possessed him and burst out upon the remote, Godless parish he had been given. His superiors thought his poor academic credentials deserved no better. *At least he can do no harm there,* they thought.

It was because of his saintly life that clearly depended on the very many hours he spent in prayer each day and night, he was made the patron of parish priests. Sadly, today, many are so taken up with mastering the means of communicating the truth that they forget what the truth is. As the Curé saw so simply, the truth is that God is love and that his love alone can change the world. This love can be communicated to others not because they are masters of modern communications or great preachers or teachers but only because they are possessed by it. Or rather, it possesses them. The forty thousand people who visited his parish were not only deeply impressed by the parish priest but by the parishioners too, who freely and lovingly opened their doors to receive them. Thanks to a man whose love first converted and then inspired a semi-pagan parish, making it into a thriving, loving Christian community, visitors encountered Christ's love in him and in the vibrant, loving family communities that first characterised the early Church. If only a fraction of the time given to criticising the Church today, no matter how she may righty deserve it, were given to receive the only power that can restore her, then what one man did for his semi-pagan parish can be done for the world through a Church that can only be renewed by prayer.

CHAPTER 45

With Thanks to My Own Family

I WENT TO A CATHOLIC SCHOOL run by secular priests, over twenty of whom I can still name to this day. I became a boarder because I, like most of the other boarders, had chosen to become a priest like those who taught us. However, although I personally liked many of these priests, I did not see them practising the personal prayer that was so deeply embedded in the one whom they had chosen for their patron saint, the Curé d'Ars; so, I decided to try my vocation as a Franciscan instead. I was surprised that at school, we were expected to spend almost half an hour in prayer before and after Mass, but those who said Mass at the high altar and the many side altars did not do the same.

Truth to tell, most of them said Mass so quickly that one of the boys used to time them. He ran a book to see who was the fastest to leave then return to the sacristy. I still remember that the usual winner was a priest who could say his Latin Mass in seventeen and a half minutes. Strangely, this did not put most of us off pursuing vocations as diocesan priests. However, it did not later surprise me when four of these priests were convicted for the sexual abuse of children, including the Rector who mainly said our daily Mass at the high altar. I suddenly saw a picture of him, fifty years later, on the BBC evening news presented as a paedophile of prodigious proportions. And the news item was correct. However, I do not want to dwell on a matter that has been written about *ad nause-am*. I merely mention it here to make two points. Firstly, that it is only those who were not alive before the Council who blame the Council for all the evils they like to think did not exist before it. The Second Vatican Council did not cause the problems but merely took the lid off the can of worms that had not yet been revealed for all to see. It had previously remained tightly sealed due to the firm, authoritative powers who ruled the Church. Such authorities were able to keep hidden what was later exposed to the masses. Several fellow students, as well as myself, came to realize that some of our teachers were what we called 'funny priests'. (And the term 'funny priests' was in no way referring to their humour!) I visited many other Catholic schools at the time to play rugby or cricket and had many friends who went to such schools; these visits and friendships enabled me to see that these 'funny priests' were not restricted to my school.

The grass was not greener when I jumped over the fence and into the Franciscan order that had come a long way since St Francis. So far, indeed, that it would never have admitted its founder into their novitiate. Far from developing the meditation that the school spiritual director had taught us, no teaching at all was given on personal prayer, either in the novitiate or the student house. When the families of Franciscan students were allowed to visit each summer, I witnessed the frightening gap that had widened between the loving families from which they had come and the new 'family' they had joined. Somehow, in some mysterious way, good Catholic families were able to retain the essence of the spirituality of love of their first Christian forebears that had been extracted from most forms of religious life after the anti-mystical witch hunts that followed in the wake of Quietism. Nor was their spirituality unduly affected by the neo-intellectualism of the Enlightenment, at least not in their spiritual lives. Yet, when their sons entered the Franciscan Order, it was not to have the heartfelt spirituality that first inspired them brought to perfection. It was to have it replaced in favour of a form of asceticism designed to generate a type of moral perfection that owed as much to the teachings of the classical Stoics as to the teaching of the Gospels. This replacement was due to the classical education that generally seeped into Christian education in the wake of the Renaissance.

When it failed as it always did, they threw themselves into the current scholastic philosophy and theology that took them into a different abstract and theoretical world to that of the loving families who visited them. It must have been a bewildering experience to see their sons become Catholic Mandarins who seemed to live in a different and rarefied atmosphere to the one in which they had brought them up. Their scholastic learning looked to Aristotle as its ultimate mentor rather than to Jesus Christ, who was the mentor of the Church Fathers, for whom theology and practical spirituality were inseparably intertwined. Along with the scriptures, Christ is the source to which we must turn, above all others, for the genuine Catholic Spirituality of love—the true tradition we must never abandon.

Even with the advent of what was called the 'New Biblical Theology', with its picturesque and pictorial teaching promising to change them, the change was only superficial, if welcome. It did not lead them on and into the profound Mystical Spirituality of Christ himself and that of the first Christians to whom he bequeathed it. It should have led them to appreciate and practise the profound personal and prayerful inner life of Christ himself and those who gave their lives and even their deaths to follow him. Instead, it sadly led to the outward expressions of the biblical theology that enthralled them.

Later, practical experience, research, and study over many years taught me that what happened to the Franciscan Order happened in all other religious orders and congregations, too, of both men and women. This loss of proper spiritual focus has inevitably led to their physical and spiritual deterioration and demise, which has been witnessed to the present day.

When religious orders and congregations fall into decline and eventually fail, it is very difficult for them to renew themselves. The family, however, is different. Grace builds on nature, and the God-given nature of human beings ensures that the mystery of this human loving continually rises, generation after generation. As human loving 'springs eternal', so does hope. This love is ignited year after year and can open the receivers to the divine love that brings it to perfection through the graces of the Sacrament of Marriage. In this way, our faith's tradition is literally handed on from its first receivers through to the families in which that tradition is practised today, perhaps in different forms but, spiritually, essentially the same. That is why I have put so much stress on the family spirituality that Christ himself gave to the early Church and which has been subtly but surely handed on to us. I have done this in detail to help purify Catholic devotional spirituality from anything that has disfigured it.

All our attention and emphasis should be placed on safeguarding, encouraging, and promoting the family, which is being attacked today like never before. All our efforts should be centred on helping Catholic families regenerate the faith they have always tried to live and hand on to their sons and daughters. If not for my own family and the profound contemplative spirituality to which they were led by the Holy Spirit, who never deserts those who earnestly seek him, I would not be writing this for you now. I write this with thanks to them and my Recusant ancestors who suffered imprisonment, torture, and death for the faith that we can so easily take for granted.

CHAPTER 46

The Whole Truth and Nothing but the Truth

WHY DID GOD DEMAND that Christ should have to suffer the most humiliating, degrading, and painful death that the Romans could devise? The simple answer is that he did not; we did. Re-read the Passion account; you will see that we fallen human beings, represented by leaders of the Jewish religion, demanded it, not God. If we were in their position, we would have done the same. If you confront anyone or any group of people with the truth—and that truth conflicts with the power, the position, and the pleasure-seeking in which they glory—then beware. For in their own time and in their own way, they will crucify you as Christ himself was crucified.

Hundreds of years before Christ, Socrates was put to death for speaking the truth the authorities did not wish to hear. In this way, he was much like the prophets in the Old Testament. They begged God not to use them as his mouthpiece because suffering and death were so often the penalty for speaking the truth. Remember, Christ himself promised that his followers would, like him, be asked to suffer and often die for the same truth that he died for—proclaiming it loud and clear (John 15:20-21, Luke 11:49-51, & Luke 21:12). The fact of the matter is that even living a good life is seen as a reproach to those who do not. If you are called to preach and teach how to live such a life to those in power and their peers, then the writing is on the wall. When you look at the battered, bruised, and bleeding body of Christ on the Cross, you are literally looking at the carnage perpetrated by evil on unalloyed goodness. You are looking at the evil of those whose hatred of him and his truth could not be satisfied by anything less than the extreme tortures, torments, and ultimate degradation of the person who threatened to unmask them.

Even today, in tyrannies throughout the world, tyrants still do to those who threaten them what was once done to Christ and those who followed him. However, in most democracies today, such extreme barbarism is thankfully unacceptable. Instead, modern hypocrites, such as the politically correct, have devised their own ways of preventing truthtellers from speaking in the first place. Even in the Church, lest Christ should speak again through others as he did before, would-be prophets currently called whistle-blowers, troublemakers, or rigid retro-traditionalists are being psychologically undermined or, to use the current terminology, simply 'cancelled' and relegated to outer darkness. Meanwhile, those who continually try to cancel them and consign them to oblivion are busily employed in remaking their god and his "truth" in their own image and likeness. Yet the truth of decline must be exposed, stated, and accepted, no matter how much the powers-that-be would like to sweep it under the carpet along with those who proclaim it. If this is not done, and not done now, for we are in the last minute of extra time, then the truth necessary for new birth and resurrection will never be heard.

If the rise of the family-based spirituality that Christ originally introduced into the early Church were depicted as a graph, then it would by and large be seen as a continuous upward line. However, after the spiritual deterioration that set in after Christianity had become the Roman Empire's official religion, that ascending graph line changed course. To the present day, and for several reasons, some of which I have described, the graph has followed a downward trend, albeit with numerous upward spikes, thanks to the great saints who have tried to return to what has been forgotten.

As the graph line gradually plummeted, characteristics notable by their absence in the early Church soon became commonplace. The first Christians were notable for their love of one another and for others, too. That notable love extended to their enemies since it was the self-same love with which Christ loved them.

But sadly, as subsequent centuries unfolded, that quality of love has sufficiently diminished for Jonathan Swift to say—and I do not hesitate to quote him again— 'We have enough religion to enable us to hate, but not enough to love one another'. The way in which so many different religions have behaved toward each other, not to mention the way they have treated their own, is scandalous. To this, the ways Christians have warred against each other, most particularly in Europe, for hundreds of years and, more recently, in two world wars, have more than confirmed what Swift had regrettably realised. That is not to mention how, instead of converting the world as Christ commanded them to do, Christians exploited it for their own financial gain, and advantage. 'You gave us the Bible', the dispossessed conceded 'but took away our lands, our possessions, and our sons and daughters'.

In general, contemporary literature remained silent about the infamy underpinning English society. In her novel *Mansfield Park*, Jane Austen insinuates that her world of wealthy landowners, decorous manners, and superficiality was possible only thanks to the greatest moral blot on English history. I am referring to the forced migration and mass degradation of hundreds of thousands of innocent Africans brutally torn from their homes and families and sold into slavery to finance the worst period of moral degradation in our secular history. And though not everyone benefited financially from this heinous 'trade', almost everyone looked the other way and failed to speak out against such terrible trafficking from which they benefitted, at least indirectly.

If wars and slavery displayed just how far Christianity had strayed from her historical origins, then sexual abuse and cover-ups have done the same in more recent history. This waywardness can clearly be seen not just from the worldwide sexual abuse of children but also by the well-documented abuse of women by priests and the abuse of young women and children by female religious. Additionally, the mutually consenting sexual relationships between priests and religious and lay men and women are still being covered up. And, before the rise of whistle-blowers, there was the almost universal silence of those 'good priests and religious' and their superiors who might not have sinned themselves but committed the sin of omission by their silence. In law, they are called 'accessories'. In the Gospels, they are called 'hypocrites' and 'whited sepulchres'.

The recently released governmental report regarding sexual abuse in Britain, in the wake of two earlier reports in Ireland, makes horrifying if salutary reading and silences the usual deniers with evidence that cannot be denied. As a resident of the United Kingdom, I leave it to others to detail the even more horrifying details of abuse in the USA if, perhaps, for no other reason than that their population is much greater than ours. What has happened in Rome is so much worse, for instead of dealing with the situation, they are actually institutionalising and sacralising what has been, from the beginning, considered mortally sinful.

Consciences brainwashed into believing that the desecration of the innocent is preferable to safeguarding the institution's reputation show, yet again, just how far our leaders have digressed from their origins. Such strayed consciences also show just how far the prayer uniting priests and religious with their Lord has long since been totally neglected. It now seems evident that a spirituality that has been stripped of the Mystical Prayer in which selfless giving is taught and that can alone turn sinners into saints through inner purification is no longer fit for purpose. When this form of prayer is ridiculed, as it is today, then so also is Christ and the Cross he carried and died upon as an example to all who would follow him (1 Corinthians 1:23-30).

CHAPTER 47

The One Thing Necessary

WHAT DO WE DO HERE AND NOW to live the spirituality Christ first gave us? Do we need Christ to come again? No, because he has never left us. Do we need the Holy Spirit's love to be poured out once more? No, because that love has never stopped pouring out. All that is needed is to start again doing what Christ himself preached and practised and what St Peter called upon the first converts to do on Pentecost day in imitation of him. We must simply keep turning to God through an ever-deepening prayer life that will enable him to do for us and through us and for 'the world in need' what nobody else can. In this way, the simplest of believers will soon find that their knowledge about what really matters here on earth infinitely surpasses that of others. These are men and women who are worshipped by the 'worldly-wise' as the great intellectual geniuses and leaders, none of whom agree with one another.

For centuries, the free thinkers of the Enlightenment have dazzled with their philosophical speculations, those with no spiritual homes to go to. It has not dawned on anyone that they have all disagreed with one another, especially about the most critical issue: the true practical wisdom we all need to live meaningful and fulfilling lives with those we love. So, how could any of them come near the Truth Christ taught in the Gospels?

They were as far away from the simple truth Christ brought as were the freethinking biblical reformers before them. They may all have had the same Bible from which to read, but each interpreted it according to an unpurified self rather than according to the inspiration of the Holy Spirit. This self-led interpretation inevitably led to what they deemed as more suitable changes in God's words and, therefore, His will. This alteration led to their opponents saying, 'Protestant: Bible in hand is his own Pope'. This accusation led to the civil war in England. In this war, ostensibly about political power, both sides were internally divided by different religious interpretations of the truth. At the war's end, they were not reconciled and were even further divided down to the present day. Christ prayed for unity and upheld that it as a sign of the Holy Spirit's presence at work in his chosen people; so, how can he be fully present in each different and dissenting sect, claiming they alone have a monopoly on true wisdom (see Luke 11:17; Mark 3:25; Matthew 12:25)?

The tragedy today is that the freethinkers in other Christian religions are now to be found in the Catholic religion, too. They are not seeking to change the world through a tradition presided over by the Holy Spirit. Instead, they seek their own self-sought 'wisdom', taken piecemeal and uncritically from a secular world still waiting for redemption. True wisdom is the gift of the Holy Spirit given to those who seek him in the purifying contemplative prayer to which all are called, but all too few choose to pursue. Because this wisdom comes from God and not man, it can be received only in the prayer that is open to all. After Christ was glorified, he returned to heaven to contemplate his Father's glory more perfectly than ever before. Then, he poured out the love he experienced in his heavenly contemplation through his human nature so that all human beings who were open to receiving it on the first Pentecost day and on every subsequent day could become wholly transformed. This transformation would take place not just by being taken up into his new glorified being but into his new contemplative loving of his Father to receive the fruits of contemplation. Perhaps the first noticeable fruit of this contemplation that comes through God's love is wisdom.

True wisdom is open to all, even the simplest who pray because it comes from a loving God and not from man. Every sincere Christian who prays daily, whether they have an IQ of 45 or 145, will receive the true God-given wisdom that does not depend on human brain power or intellectual learning, as the lives of the saints make abundantly clear. The dunce of the class can know more about the love of God than the greatest of Nobel prize winners. This is the only wisdom that can change our lives permanently for the better, as well as the world we are committed to serving in Christ's name.

Just as St Francis of Assisi would not have the qualifications to join the Franciscan Order today, nor would the Curé d'Ars have the qualifications to enter a seminary today; yet they both had the one thing necessary. Sadly, this seems to be the one thing that is optional or only nominally necessary for contemporary priests and religious. If deep personal prayer had been their staple daily diet, then the vast catalogue of sexual abuse and coverups could not possibly have occurred.

Although the Breviary is said and the Divine Office is chanted in priories and friaries and monasteries, the psalms that are the heart and soul of these liturgies are but the outward expression of an inner personal relationship with God. Without the love of God that is first learnt and developed in personal prayer, the recitation or singing of the psalms can soon become a meaningless daily treadmill to be 'got through' as quickly as possible, if it is said at all. Or even worse, it can become a sort of spiritual concert, even a charade. It may well attract believers and non-believers alike and win their admiration due to the place where it is celebrated and because its intrinsic aesthetic beauty makes them feel spiritually uplifted. However, if it is not the outward expression of the love of

God learnt by each individual in personal prayer before the liturgy begins, then, as St Paul put it, it will soon become no more than gongs booming and cymbals clashing. Those who celebrate liturgy without love use words and actions that are not so much inspired by their need to be pleasing to God but rather to be pleasing to the congregation for whom they are primarily performing their stylised celebrations. In short, they are performing an act of communal hypocrisy. To avoid this happening to his brothers, St Bernadine of Siena wrote these words in letters of gold around the choir stalls where his brothers recited the divine office: *Si cor non orat in vanum lingua laborat* (If the heart does not pray, then the tongue labours in vain). He was merely reminding his brothers what Christ himself taught his disciples in his day by quoting the words of Isaiah: 'These people worship me with their lips, but their hearts are far from me' (Matthew 15:8-9 & Isaiah 29:13).

The dissolute and corrupt state of Judaism in Christ's day mirrors the similar state of Catholicism in our day due to the demise of the deep personal prayer that Christ and his first followers in the early Church practised. It is no good continually trying to sweep under the carpet the vast numbers of priests and religious, who, despite saying or singing their liturgies, seriously offended their vow of chastity in one despicable form or another, either by action or omission. Nor is it believable that these betrayals are all behind us now. Such betrayals will be repeated until practitioners teach the daily prayer that leads through purification to union with God. This prayer practice must become a normal part of priestly and religious formation, otherwise such betrayals will be repeated. Remember Einstein's definition of insanity: *Doing the same thing over and over again and expecting different results.*

The way forward is not to change the outward expressions of our faith handed down to us through tradition, nor to replace it with the latest superficial fads and fancies, but to reanimate it from within. This reanimation can be done only by the power and presence of the Holy Spirit, who can alone re-enliven and re-invigorate those who are languishing to death without his transforming presence. It is only through those who have rededicated their lives to receive him that the transformation which we yearn for more than anything else can be brought about. This rededication must be embodied in the personal daily prayer, without which all else will fail. As Christ himself said, this and this alone is 'the one thing necessary'.

CHAPTER 48

Introducing Two of My Main Mentors

IF YOU ASKED CATHOLICS TO VOTE for their favourite saint, chances are ten to one that St Anthony of Padua would come out on top because of his uncanny way of finding lost items. Ironically, he became a Franciscan only because he could not find his own way to North Africa and ended up in Italy instead. It was St Francis who was so impressed by his learning that he called him 'my theologian' and set him to work educating his friars for the rest of his life. He was such a great theologian that, to this day, the Franciscan University in Rome is called The Antonianum in his honour. Here, in the late 1950s, a young Franciscan called Ignatius Kelly OFM received one of the highest theological degrees ever granted. It was called a *summa cum laude* (with the highest distinction), and he was carried in triumph by his fellow students. At almost the same time, and unknown to most of her fans, the hermit, Sr Wendy Beckett, received a similar distinction in English at Oxford. When she walked into her final oral examination, her professors stood up to applaud her, for no other student had ever received such high marks. Both of them had a decisive influence on my life and my writing.

Five years after I graduated, I was appointed as the Director of a retreat and conference centre in London for twelve years. It was to Fr Ignatius that I turned as my principal and most popular speaker. Unfortunately, his brilliant theology was not matched by a succession of pious but incompetent priests who failed abysmally to teach us spiritual theology. That is why I asked Fr Ignatius to give a course on Mystical Theology. Without a moment's thought, he responded, 'I know nothing whatsoever about Mystical Theology'. I was horrified.

Almost fifty years later, I am still looking for theology professors, theologians, and Catholic academics who have both practical experience of and detailed knowledge about the inner spiritual journey that leads through purification to union with God. Although there must be thousands of Professors of theology and academic theologians, their silence is deafening when the Church is presently in her hour of need.

If they were full practitioners in what they profess, they would not only have true wisdom instead of just academic knowledge, but they would also have the inner spiritual strength to speak out against the Machiavellian moral malaise currently threatening to destroy the Church. Even the most distinguished academic geniuses are blind and, therefore, helpless until mystical purification removes their spiritual cataracts from their eyes so they can see with infused wisdom what they could not see before. They would then receive the power to proclaim it, fearless of the consequences.

From St Bernard of Clairvaux (1090-1153) to the condemnation of the pseudo-mysticism called Quietism (1687), there were hundreds of great mystical theologians, writers, and practitioners. It was they who led Catholics through the spiritual purification necessary before the deeper union with God that imparts wisdom and all the other infused virtues to those sufficiently purified.

Since the anti-mystical ethos that then spread through the Catholic Church to ensure that false mysticism would never rise again, Catholic mystical writers and practitioners have all but disappeared.

Aided and abetted by a neo-rationalism that seeped into Catholic theology and spirituality resulting from the 'Enlightenment', the ancient Catholic teaching of dying to self by daily carrying the cross, learnt in Mystical Prayer under the influence and guidance of the Holy Spirit, has been all but forgotten. Furthermore, Mystical Prayer was, and still is, greeted with hostility by laity, priests, and religious alike. This hostility is particularly true of those who have inherited the anti-mystical ethos that still prevails amongst Catholics brought up and educated in what has been called 'the first world'.

The hostility found before was totally absent when I was asked to lecture to indigenous religious in the 'third world' in four major tours to equatorial Africa. When I was speaking to about one hundred members of a fairly new African religious congregation, the Little Sisters of St Francis, at their mother house a few miles north of Lake Victoria in Uganda, something momentous happened. I was in the middle of introducing the teaching of St John of the Cross and St Teresa of Avila in order to explain how the Holy Spirit prepares all who would persevere in prayer beyond first beginnings when I misinterpreted the room's atmosphere. I thought it was yet again a particular hostility to which I had become accustomed in the 'first world' where my teaching was usually dismissed as 'for the birds'. My confidence got the better of me, and I stopped in mid-sentence to ask, 'I am so sorry. Am I making sense?' I will never forget the response.

The silence that I thought was indicating a certain lack of understanding, if not disapproval, was nothing of the kind. Simultaneously, every head in the room not only nodded to express that they were hanging on every word but that they wanted me to carry on without delay. As I discovered later, it was not just that they were enthralled about a subject that no one had spoken to them about before. I was explaining to them something about which they had personal experience, but so far, no instruction. This revelation was confirmed in many subsequent private consultations. These sisters were totally free of the anti-mystical ethos with which religious in the 'first world' had been unknowingly brainwashed into believing that Mystical Theology was perilous, an extraordinary way for a chosen few and fraught with dangers. I was not surprised then but gratified that when Rome itself and the Pope who presides over the Church gave universal permission to bless serious sexual sins, that it was African bishops alone who spoke with one voice against it.

I was invited to Equatorial Africa four times, and I would still be returning had I not succumbed to tropical diseases, one of which very nearly killed me. It was this, plus my exposure to the sexual abuse I heard about during my lecture tours in Europe, that forced me to turn to writing so I could do what I could no longer do as a travelling speaker. Whistle-blowers who do not know their place must be replaced.

If it were not for a letter that I received from Sr Wendy Beckett supporting my stance in all that I wrote in the 'Catholic Herald' and the 'Catholic Universe', I might well have given up what I am still doing thanks to her friendship and her encouragement. For almost thirty years and ten books later, I am still trying to promote the profound Mystical Spirituality Christ himself practised before introducing it through his Apostles into the early Church. In the early Church years, the Risen Christ was the only source and centre of Christian spirituality. The Renaissance (beginning circa 1350) introduced Pelagian Stoicism into Catholic spirituality—due to moral teachers such as Socrates, Seneca, and Marcus Aurelius—with its own DIY asceticism. Catholic humanists introduced these moral teachers into Christian education, merging their teaching with that of Christ to produce a new moral syncretism that has been confusing the faithful down to the present day, as it confused me at school.

Christianity is not primarily a moral theology that presents us with a plethora of moral standards we can never possibly maintain; it is a Mystical Theology that gives us the power to do even the impossible. For even the impossible becomes possible when our purification enables Christ to live in us and do, in and through us, what he did for those who met him in person while he was on earth.

CHAPTER 49

Lead Kindly Light

ANYONE WHO IS COMMITTED TO THE SPIRITUAL LIFE eventually discovers that, although they travel by faith and so cannot see where they are going, they are indeed being led. They will be able to see that they have been led all along by a kindly light 'despite the encircling gloom'. At the time, they might have felt that 'the night was dark and they were far from home', unable to see 'the distant scene', making one laborious step at a time. However, with hindsight, they realise they have been led by Someone who was, despite their feelings to the contrary, always close to them.

I was battling on in the Franciscan novitiate, being severely tempted to give up the journey that seemed terribly complicated, so dark, and so meaningless. Now with hindsight, I can see the truth, which I could not see then. I received a classical education in which the Stoicism taught from Socrates of Athens to Marcus Aurelius of Rome was taught alongside with the Christianity taught by Jesus of Nazareth. The confusion that obfuscated a clear and coherent understanding of the Gospel truths was seamlessly continued in the novitiate in the instructions we were given and in the small library that had been carefully selected. There were no books on prayer to help complement the instructions on meditation and contemplation that were never given by the Novice Master nor by the Student Master in the years that followed. Instead, the little library was full of books on the virtues with which we had to adorn ourselves if we were to make ourselves into perfect Christians and exemplary religious.

Therefore, could I be blamed if I wrote down a list of all the main virtues promising to make me into the saint of my dreams? I then ordered all the virtues by priority and decided to dedicate each month of the novitiate to attain them all, each in turn, month by month. I would begin with 'humility', which seemed to be the foundation of all the other virtues, at least according to the Christian Stoics. After two months of trying to master the virtue of humility, I failed abysmally. Far from becoming more like St Francis of Assisi, I became more and more like Uriah Heap. When I failed to adorn myself with three more virtues in as many months, I knew I would either must become a better actor or receive some sort of supernatural help to do what was quite beyond me. After praying repeatedly 'Lead, Kindly Light', two minor miracles saved me from disaster.

I believe the first mini miracle came thanks to the meditation that I learnt from my school spiritual director. He insisted that progress in the spiritual life would be made only with endless and daily perseverance, which I tried to maintain in my prayer life, after supper at school, and in the chapel after compline prayers in the novitiate. Despite my evident failure to make myself into the saint of my dreams, by my Trojan efforts to master the virtues during the day, perseverance in two hours of praying each evening came to the rescue. More precisely, it was 'the kindly light' who led me, despite the 'encircling gloom,' in which I found myself when 'Acquired Contemplation' led me into *the real thing* shortly after Ash Wednesday. *The real thing* was dark and dismal and full of distractions compared with the sweetness and light I had experienced in meditation. However, unknown to me, the Holy Spirit was on my case and beginning to change my life, starting with two minor miracles. I was just putting back into the noviciate library volume I of

The Practice of Christian & Religious Perfection by Alphonsus Rodriguez SJ (this dry and dreary work detailed the virtues in three dull and doleful volumes) when I noticed something. It was whilst I was putting it back that I discovered a small spiritual masterpiece that had fallen behind an ancient tome on Canon law, thus hiding itself from the censors who wanted us to concentrate on books on the virtues, which, according to the novice master, were conspicuous by their absence in our lives.

The little book was entitled simply *Pax Animae*. The author was a Franciscan priest called John of Bonilla; another Franciscan, Dominic Devas, translated from Spanish into English. On the very first page, I read the words that began my conversion from the hybrid Christianity in which I was brought up at school and into which I was to be further educated in the Franciscan novitiate. The words were simply these: 'With God's Love, all things are possible, but without it, nothing is possible'. Within a few days, there was another minor miracle. The Franciscan priest, Fr Dominic Devas, who had translated the little gem that I kept by my bedside, was not only still alive and well and a member of our province, but he would be coming to give us our retreat! I could hardly sleep from the joy and anticipation of what was to make an otherwise miserable novitiate the turning point in my life.

He not only spoke with a conviction and wisdom that was never heard again in a retreat, but he prayed for hours in the church each day, lost in the profound contemplation he taught as the completion of the life of prayer. Far from being a sign of God's displeasure with me, the spiritual darkness in which I found myself was, in fact, the beginning of contemplation in which I had to be purified by the Holy Spirit. The distractions and temptations plaguing me were to be viewed not as obstacles but as opportunities to practise loving God when I seemed to receive nothing in return. I was taught to persevere, come hell or high water, trying to offer myself to God, sacrificing my time in endless acts of self-sacrificial giving, in imitation of the self-sacrificial giving that Christ offered to his Father whilst he was on earth. This perseverance is the only way pure, selfless loving is learnt.

In what is called *Purifying Contemplation*, a person is being prepared to be united with Christ's perfect contemplation through an ongoing inner spiritual cleansing. This purification that begins in darkness and gradually leads to heart-felt light when a preliminary purification enables a searcher to experience transitory glimpses of God's infinite love. All this occurs in, with and through Christ, in which purification eventually enables a would-be mystic to share in the praise, thanksgiving, and adoration that Christ himself continually offers to his Father. But what we have tried to do in words, prayers, songs, and psalms, Christ does in an unutterable stillness when words give way to silence. Words unite those who are separate, but in perfect union, silence reigns supreme to say what can be said only in silent loving—in what is called *contemplation*.

Our destiny, beginning here on earth, is to be purified by the love of the Holy Spirit so that we can be taken up into Christ's silent, all-consuming contemplation of his Father. Just as Christ's contemplation gives glory to his Father, so the Father gives glory to his Son and to those who pray in, with, and through him. God's glory is the mystical expression of his love. This love contains within it all the infused virtues that made Christ perfect and will make those who follow him into perfect human beings; this is an accomplishment our Stoical endeavours can never achieve.

It took two more years of drudgery in contemplative purification before light followed my darkness, but that (as many books irritatingly conclude) is another story!

CHAPTER 50

The Retreat that Changed My Life

THE RETREAT THAT CHANGED MY LIFE in the novitiate given by Fr Dominic Devas OFM made sense of what had seemed senseless before. Far from being the first to fail to make myself perfect by acquiring all the virtues, I was just the most recent. All the Stoics before me had failed. In fact, Epictetus, the founder of Stoicism, said, 'In my old age, please show me a Stoic, for I have yet to see one'. However, when the Renaissance brought Stoicism to the attention of Catholics looking for a new way to achieve perfection through their own endeavour, many turned to the Stoics for inspiration, as I did.

When I told Fr Dominic about my spiritual journey, he asked to see the list I had made of the virtues that I swore to attain before my first profession. 'There are three virtues missing', he told me, 'and, furthermore, they are the most important virtues of all. They are the three theological virtues given to us by God'. Without them, no one can possibly attain the others, and that is why the Stoics can never succeed in any age. They are Faith, Hope, and Love. But as St Paul insists, the greatest of all of them is Love. Love is the most important because it is only through love that we can come to love Christ, whose Mystical Body we have been incorporated into at Baptism. Then, our love is deepened only through coming to know him through meditation. We can then enter more deeply into him,

217

not just into his being but into his acting and into his loving of his Father.

But as our unpurified love is totally incapable of doing this, meditation ends abruptly, and the Holy Spirit leads us into the beginnings of contemplation. It is here that our love must be sufficiently purified to be fitted into Christ's own perfect contemplation of God. Here, we must persevere, no matter how terrible the darkness may seem, nor how exacting the distractions and the temptations may become. This necessary perseverance is most particularly true of the temptation to think that we are wasting our time and would be better employed in some more tangible and more satisfying form of apostolic endeavour. 'Our world', Fr Dominic said, 'is full of unpurified apostles who believe that what they are doing is for the honour and glory of God, when it is for the honour and glory of themselves'.

After many months of this purification in darkness, or more likely after several years, God's light will suddenly and dramatically banish the darkness. God, who has so far been engaged in purifying the would-be mystic, suddenly makes his presence felt in what St Teresa of Avila in her masterwork, *Interior Castle,* called 'The Prayer of Quiet'; his presence is subsequently felt in what she later calls 'The Prayer of Full Union'. In The Prayer of Quiet, God's love is experienced more powerfully than ever despite a few distractions that may remain active. However, in The Prayer of Full Union, there are no distractions, for the person who prays is so wrapped in God's love that they have no distractions at all, nor can they move, for they are rivetted to the place where they are at prayer. As God's love overflows into a human being and then into their human acting, the theological virtue of Love enables a person to cling to God. It also overflows onto and into the other theological virtues.

The faith that seemed so feeble and febrile in purification has never been stronger, and the receiver now knows without a shadow of a doubt that God exists. They know that no matter what happens in future, they can never again doubt the existence of God. Nor can they doubt that what they have experienced is His infinite loving, albeit in proportions sufficient for a finite human being to experience it without complete capitulation. If their newfound faith is not yet ready to move mountains, then it will move all obstacles that would prevent the total abandonment to God in the future. Hope that was tempted to fall into hopelessness in the darkest moments of purification now 'springs eternal'. Now, belief in eternal life knows no bounds because a part of the payment of eternal life has been received and experienced. That is why the Greek word for hope is *arrabón*, meaning *a part payment or a first instalment*.

At the same time as God's love reinvigorates the theological virtues, so also does His love reinvigorate the moral virtues; or more precisely, they are reinvigorated through the person who could not attain them before. Because they are now filled with the experience of God's love, the moral virtues are infused with that love as they begin to practise them in a way that was not possible before. That is why they came to be known as the infused moral virtues, just as the first three God-given virtues came to be known as the infused theological virtues.

Perhaps the first infused virtue that is noticed when God's love overflows into the moral virtues is the virtue of wisdom. For the first time, a believer begins to perceive God's plan for the world, for themselves and for others as they have never seen it before, and they presume that everyone will be pleased to know it, too. However, when they begin to share it with others, they are surprised to find that more than just cold water is poured on them.

In chapter seven of his work, *The Republic*, Plato pictures the majority of humanity as prisoners bound in a cave. They are positioned so that they can see only shadows of the real world depicted on the back wall of their prison. When a prisoner who is freed to see the real world outside returns to 'enlighten' his erstwhile comrades, all hell is let loose. They not only refuse to listen to him, for they are addicted to the world of shadows, but they put him to death. Plato was obviously thinking of his mentor, Socrates; what happened to him has and will happen to others who, thanks to God's love, are given the gift of infused wisdom.

Lest we conclude that the first experience of God's love is the summit of the Mystic Way, Fr Devas said that it is not the end, but only the beginning of the end of purification since after a few weeks of light and 'enlightenment', darkness returns to be followed by further light and 'enlightenment' in God's good time and not in ours. And for those who persevere, the spiritual roller coaster continues. Before Heaven can return permanently, the Hell deep down in the nether regions of our personalities fuelling the seven deadly sins must be destroyed at their source. Consequently, what St John of the Cross called 'The Dark Night of the Senses' must be followed by the 'Dark Night of the Spirit' before what St Teresa of Avila calls the 'Mystical Marriage' or the 'Transforming Union' can herald the birth of a new person.

In this person, the person of Christ can be seen living and loving as he did whilst he was on earth. What the Stoics failed to achieve was fully lived and practised by the early Christians, who were amongst the first converts to give their lives over to the only One who could redeem them.

CHAPTER 51

Marriage and Mystical Loving

ALTHOUGH I SPENT YEARS STUDYING Mystical Theology, it was, in fact, from my parents that I came to understand the meaning of the 'Mystic Way.' After My mother died, my father told me that in the last years of their married life together, he and my mother loved each other more deeply and more perfectly than at any other time in their lives. In the first days of what he described as their adolescent love, they were drawn to each other by powerful waves of emotional and passionate feelings, which inevitably faded away. My father told me that what happened between the fading of these powerful emotional feelings and the development of perfect love they experienced at the end of their lives made this perfect love possible.

For many years—no, decades—unknown to onlookers, unseen even to their closest friends, they persevered in practising selfless, sacrificial loving whether they felt like it or not, come hell or high water. It was this other-considering loving that gradually enabled them to bond ever more closely. This exchange continued until a union as perfect as possible in this life was the joy of their last years together. The first enthusiasm in human loving is clearly visible to the lovers themselves and to onlookers, too. However, the daily and ongoing self-sacrificial loving that makes any marriage is not. In the Greek that was used by the majority in the early Church, the word for *hidden, unseen, or invisible* was *mystical*. This term describes the selfless, self-sacrificial loving practised by married couples.

Be clear about this: the word *mystical* for Christians primarily means firstly and above all else – *the selfless, sacrificial loving a person practises in marriage or in a person's personal prayer life, or rather both.* Beware, therefore, because the word *mystical,* or *mysticism,* tends to be used in modern times by those not so much seeking to follow Christ by learning how to carry the cross through daily self-sacrificial love practised in marriage and in prayer beyond first beginnings but, instead, by spiritual bounty hunters. Such persons seek mostly instant esoteric supernatural experiences for their own solace and satisfaction by employing man-made methods and techniques. The word *mysticism* cannot be found in the teaching of the early Fathers of the Church because their spirituality is totally God-centred. They all taught how to seek God through selfless giving, not magic. As Greek ceased to be the predominant language used by the majority of Christians, the word *mystical* was no longer used to describe married loving but only the hidden or unseen loving of those lay, married, and celibate Christians who sought God in an ever-deepening personal prayer life.

My mother said that if she and my father had not already been married, then their marriage could have easily floundered and failed. She was referring to the spiritual marriage they had both entered when they were baptised. This, their marriage to Christ, gave them access to God's grace that continually sustained and supported their weak human love. As she later explained, her marriage's success depended on this other marriage and on the spiritual or mystical loving first learnt there, even before she walked down the aisle with her husband. This loving learnt gradually opened them both to receive the mystical loving of God that would gradually mingle, mix, and merge with their own weak human love. This mingling would not only enable them to love God more deeply but each other, too, and, ultimately, all the children that they were given. Each of them, in their own deeply personal and spiritual journeys that would manifest themselves most particularly in prayer, would, like Christ the first Mystic, have to experience what it felt like when God seemed far away, and terrible temptations and distractions would all but overcome them.

This darkness is what Christ had to experience in the desert, in the garden of Gethsemane, and on the Cross. However, there would be other moments when he would be overwhelmed with joy as he prayed with his own family, his disciples, and with his apostles on Mount Tabor. St John of the Cross would describe such darkness in his book, *Dark Night of the Soul*, and St Teresa of Avila would describe the joy when darkness was replaced by the light of God's presence in her masterwork, *Interior Castle*. What she describes there can be found at the very beginning of Christianity as experienced by St Paul, when he wrote about the visions and revelations that he received when he was raised into what he called the 'third heaven', which he identified with paradise regained (2 Corinthians 12:1-5). This level of heaven is described by St Teresa of Avila and called the prayer of 'Full Union' or even 'Ecstasy' in her famous mystical masterpiece. This Mystical Prayer that St Teresa of Avila called the very soul of the Church is now under serious and systematic attack.

If I had told my parents that they were mystics, they would have laughed. Like so many other parents who had to battle against 'the slings and arrows of outrageous fortune' to find the peace they finally attained, they were indeed mystics. They were quite clearly married mystics from whom celibates called to the Mystic Way could well learn what they have long since forgotten. This loving is also called *mystical* for a Christian because it takes place in and continues to grow within the Mystical Body of Jesus Christ, where it is united with Christ's own mystical loving or his contemplation of his Father that he practised while he was on earth and is now brought to perfection as he is in heaven. The body of knowledge gathered together and recorded by those who have travelled along the Mystic Way to help others is called Mystical Theology or Mystical Spirituality. It details the selfless, sacrificial loving practised in personal prayer when first fervour fizzles out in the spiritual life, as it does in married life. Mystical Theology is the result, the consequence, or byproduct of selfless, sacrificial loving, not of self-sought techniques or magical man-made methods promising instant mystical experiences.

CHAPTER 52

In the Trying Is the Dying

PRAYER IS FOR A CHRISTIAN what a gymnasium is for an athlete. The muscles of your heart, rather than the body, are exercised as they practise what is called 'weight training' or 'pumping iron'. The principle behind it is straightforward: by repeatedly raising weights above your head in the gymnasium, you are not just developing the muscles in your arms and legs, but virtually every other muscle in your body as well in one simple action. The whole person is not only made stronger and more powerful but is given powers of endurance beyond those who do not use this method.

The same holds true in the spiritual gymnasium, which is prayer. What is prayer but the raising of the heart and mind to God? It is just like weight training. Whatever form of prayer you are engaged in, whether it is saying your morning prayers, trying to meditate, or even contemplating, you will always experience distractions. Therefore, you will always have to keep raising your heart and mind to God time and time again. As a person does this, the spiritual heart and mind muscles are continually being exercised, thus gradually transforming the whole spiritual metabolism. Athletes know that this concentrated period of physical exercise will enable greater ease and facility to whatever they do in the rest of their day. The same is true for the spiritual athlete. They and others, too, will benefit from the love generated in prayer, where the spiritual heart muscles are developed more quickly and more fully than anywhere else.

There is no time like the present. This journey can begin now in what Jean-Pierre de Caussade SJ called 'the sacrament of the present moment', where alone time can touch eternity. Never be deceived into believing that continual failures will disqualify us from this journey. God judges us by how best we try no matter how many times we fall, for only he knows the power of our personal 'demons' and how best we have tried to overcome them. Everyone begins life with a different hand of cards. Everyone begins with different parents or only one or even none. Even the best of parents are themselves psychologically handicapped by what nature and nurture have failed to give them and what we, therefore, have failed to receive from them. But remember, God ultimately judges us by how best we have tried despite the odds which have been seemingly against us from the beginning. And he also judges those who have received so much yet have given so little. Only God knows the quality of our endeavour in comparison with what we were given at the beginning of our life, so only he can judge us at the end of it by how best we have tried. He judges us not by what the world may think we have achieved but by what he knows we have achieved. There is an old Spanish proverb that says, 'You see what I drink, but you do not see my thirst'. God does!

Only Our Lady was conceived without sin, meaning that the rest of us were not. Consequently, we are continually falling, both inside and outside of prayer, whether we like it or not. That includes the saints, too. The difference between us and the saints is not that they did not sin, but we do. They sinned just as we do. What distinguishes the saint from the sinner is the speed with which they get up after falling. The saints do not waste precious time pretending they do not sin or making endless excuses or blaming others for what they know only too well was their own fault. When passing through Purgatory, Dante noticed that now, at last, people saw the truth so they did not spend their time blaming others but only themselves for the sins separating them from God. The saints recognised their culpability even in this life. The moment they fell, they did not waste time blaming others but only themselves and so they sought forgiveness and began again, knowing they had sinned yet trusting God's mercy.

Herein lies one of the main differences between the saints and sinners like us. Too often, people simply cannot face their guilt, so they run away from God and hide, as Adam did in the Garden of Eden. When God called out, 'Adam, Adam, where are you?' (Genesis 3:9), God knew exactly where Adam was: Adam did not know where he was. He had lost his way, trying to hide his sin and the guilt that shamed him. Sometimes, we can spend years on the run because pride will not allow us to admit what we have done. Our inability to eat humble pie means we can spend half a lifetime suffering from spiritual starvation. What is even worse than the pride that comes before a fall is the pride that follows the fall because it stops us from getting up, sometimes permanently.

Whether in or out of prayer, the measure of spiritual advancement can always be determined by the speed with which we turn back to God from the distractions, the temptations, or the sins that try to turn us away from him. However, all the saints discovered that this speed can only be maintained with help and strength from God.

That is why, although they may have differed from one another in everything else, they were one in their daily commitment to prayer. They knew without a shadow of a doubt that without it, they had no power to do anything of any real value or worth, let alone advance in the spiritual life. Consequently, each of them, in different ways, echoed the words of St Teresa of Avila when she said, 'There is only one way to perfection, and that is to pray. If anyone points in another direction, then they are deceiving you'.

The very essence of our spiritual journey, then, is in endlessly getting up no matter how many times we fall. It is in this, more than anything else, that the real quality of our love is measured. Even if we do not initially have a pure and humble heart, a pure and humble heart will be God's gift for those who persevere in following their heart's desire, come what may. The most pernicious stumbling block to our spiritual advancement is the pride following our fall, which induces us to pack up and run away from God rather than face the truth of our sinfulness. Yet again, I insist that the difference between the saint and the sinner is not that they never fail as we do but the speed with which they seek forgiveness and begin again immediately, no matter how many times they fall. This perseverance takes great humility and is how true humility is learned.

When you stop falling, you are in heaven, but when you stop getting up, you will be in hell. In the trying is the dying, and in the dying is the rising that draws us up into the Mystical Body of Christ and into his Mystical Contemplation of his Father.

–Peter Calvay, Hermit

CHAPTER 53

The Sacrament of Marriage

A HIGHLY EDUCATED LAYMAN, with more Catholic credentials than I ever came across before, made a statement which simply poleaxed me. He said that he could not understand why, after being baptised by the Holy Spirit in the River Jordon, Christ rushed off to the wedding of an unknown couple at a remote village called Cana in Galilee. Why this unnecessary diversion? Why did he not forego what the layman deemed a secular celebration that usually ended up in overindulgence anyway, to go without delay to preach the coming of God's Kingdom? Furthermore, why should Pope St John Paul II make it the second of the new Luminous Mysteries of the Rosary in 2002? His misunderstanding must be addressed lest others make the same mistake and misunderstand a vital sacrament without which God's plan could not be implemented after Christ's Glorification. Let me explain.

The promise made to Abraham to make a great nation out of his seed and the promise of a Messiah to lead them totally depended on the families who would be instrumental in fulfilling this promise. No families—no future. That is why the rite of circumcision, by which the means of bringing about more people to populate this new nation, was a sacred rite. The need for families is also why, in the Old Testament, those who could not procreate were considered cursed by God.

Christ purposely chose to go to this wedding at Cana before all else to recognise this sacred sacrament of the Old Testament; additionally, he desired to draw attention to and sacralise in advance what would become the great sacrament of the New Testament. Marriage would become the basis of the new religion he founded. It would become the setting in which new Christians would be born, nurtured, and taught by word and example to love in a new way in families borne not from human conception alone but by a new conception of the Holy Spirit when they were baptised. Christ's ever-present and all-consuming loving would support and sustain them through the other sacraments for the rest of their lives.

In those first Christian centuries, they believed in this love and that they could access it with their vital living faith. This faith induced them and their families to renounce everything that was preventing them from abandoning themselves to receive this supernatural loving every moment of every day of their lives. Unfortunately, today, after thousands of years, the Church has become so moribund with institutionalism, formalism and the accompanying nominalism that what was once a vital living faith has, for the majority, become little more than a ceremonial faith. The same Creed is still recited, but what was the clarion call to daily action for first Christians is now no more than another rather tedious expression of their cultural identity for today's churchgoers. If in the early Church, five percent were nominal Catholics and ninety-five percent were as active as the apostles who inspired them, then today, these figures would have to be reversed.

The only way such figures can be reversed is by a gigantic reawakening in which believers can once more believe in the massive spiritual fusion of divine energy being poured out of Christ. Believers must ask with all earnestness and with practical intent how to receive this spiritual energy. Today's believers must receive the same answer given to the first Christians who acted on what they were told with an ongoing immediacy that changed the world. They had to learn how to love the God whose love was always loving them with His own infinite loving. Look no further than to the person of Christ, for it was in loving him alone that they could open themselves to receive his love in return.

Consequently, meditation became the first step towards generating personal love for Christ as he was on earth so that this love could be redirected to loving him now as he is in heaven. This meditation led to a deeper and more profound form of praying in, with and through Christ, called Mystical Contemplation. Contemplation always begins in darkness because God's infinite loving highlights the evil within us, which is separating us from the goodness in him. If we are prepared to persevere in prayer for many months or rather years, only then can our desire to love God be so purified that we can begin to receive what alone can change us: our families and those other families whom Christ wants to reach out to through us. That this mystical purification took place so widely and deeply in the early Church is clearly evident from the massive conversions that the Holy Spirit was able to bring about, working through those who were sufficiently purified to receive him.

Although without them realising it, in contemplation, believers learn like never before to take up their daily cross by dying to self in what came to be called *white martyrdom*. Here, a habit of selfless giving is learnt. This habit of selfless loving enables them to receive in ever greater fullness the infinite loving that overflows into their families, into their work, and into everything they say or do each day. When everyone in the Church is united in doing this together, then the families set afire by love become the beacons from which Christ's light can transform the world. Thus, the family was and always will be the setting from which God's love reaches out to set the Church and, ultimately, the world afire with the only love that can be its salvation.

Accepting the invitation to the marriage feast at Cana was not Christ's way of making merry after enduring suffering in the desert. Nor was it his attempt to take advantage of a diversion before the arduous task of teaching and preaching in the months ahead. His attendance at the wedding was far more than that. He (along with his holy mother) was celebrating the great sacrament that enabled God's promise to Abraham to be fulfilled through human loving. At the same time, the wedding was a symbolic promise of a new and far more profound sacrament to bring about God's new plans, not just for one race but for the whole of the human race.

The other Gospel writers might have called the transformation of water into wine a miracle (which indeed it was), but St John calls it a sign. This transformation is a sign of the new sacrament of love in which human love would be suffused and surcharged with divine love. In other words, it would far surpass the old sacrament's inner dynamism as wine's inner dynamism surpasses that of water. The new sacrament of marriage would put the family and the human, and the divine love generated therein as the foundation and consummation of the love that would spread throughout and bond together the new Kingdom of God on earth.

The families that prayed together did stay together. They conquered the pagan world with the love of Christ, who was born again in their holy families through the same Holy Spirit who brought him to birth at Bethlehem.

CHAPTER 54

When You Stop Falling, You Will Be in Heaven

A WHILE AGO, I WENT TO A SPECIAL MASS prepared by a group of laypeople to ask for God's mercy on them and on their families as part of their preparation for Lent. The readings, the psalms, and the prayers had all been chosen to echo the overall theme of asking God to give his loving mercy to all those present and to the whole world that would be lost without it. The visiting preacher came straight to the point. 'Why waste your time praying for God's loving mercy?' he asked. 'Whether you pray for it or not, his loving mercy has been sent out, is being sent out, and will continue to be sent out, whether you pray for it or not. Why not save your breath to cool your porridge? Or rather save your breath to pray that we will be given the strength to take the steps to receive it, by finding time to do so in our daily lives.'

In the Old Testament, the word *hesed* was used to describe the loving mercy of God. In the New Testament, it has been translated by the Latin word *gratia*, which gave birth to the English word *grace*. Fortunately, nothing is lost in translation; in fact, everything is gained. Now that the Holy Spirit has been and is continually being sent, his love is no longer referred to as *hesed* but *gratia* or grace. This *hesed*, this *gratia* is the same love of God that revolved between the Father and the Son from and to eternity. But now, thanks to the Glorified Christ, he sends it out to do something that was never

233

needed to be done before. For now, its power to forgive sins is seen, as this love is directed to sinful human beings to dispel the sinfulness that would otherwise keep God out.

That is why all the sacraments give grace, God's loving mercy that first forgives the sins that would otherwise prevent him from making his home within us as he promised at the Last Supper. There is only one thing that can prevent God from making his home within us: the sickness of sin and selfishness that does to the Mystical Body of Christ what high cholesterol does to the physical body. It must ultimately be controlled, if not totally rooted out.

In one way or another, we all must be purified of the selfishness that prevents the pure love of God from possessing us. The spiritual life is a journey from selfishness to selflessness because only a selfless person can become one with the utterly Selfless One, who is all-pure, undiluted loving. This transformation from selfishness to selflessness is a lengthy business that will be commensurate with the whole of our lives. Unless we make a genuine attempt to rid ourselves of the selfishness that keeps God out, then we will make no spiritual progress. Unless we try to change our self-centred lives outside of prayer, our prayer itself will never develop beyond the most rudimentary stages. Even from a psychological viewpoint, if we have behaved badly all day, then prayer will be quite impossible at the day's end. In fact, one of the reasons why people run away from prayer is that they know it will mean coming to terms with themselves and doing something about their shoddy lifestyles.

Even though we may make the Morning Offering as sincerely as possible and genuinely try to implement it in the forthcoming day, we will fail unless something is done to cure the scourge of selfishness impeding our best intentions and our sincerest efforts. God wants us to do all within our power to strip away everything in our lives that is preventing us from uniting ourselves with Him at each and every moment of our lives. Only then will he be able to possess us as fully as he has planned. If we do not see the sin and selfishness preventing our growth in the spiritual life, it is not because we are sinless, it is simply because we are blind. We must cry out with Bartimaeus: 'Lord, that I may see' (Mark 10:46-52).

In one of the most memorable retreats I have ever attended, Archbishop Anthony Bloom began by telling the story of a retired headmistress who offered him her services as a chauffeur. As they were returning home one Monday afternoon, she stopped the car in Kensington to pick up her new glasses from the opticians and proceeded to try them out for the remainder of the journey. The journey was less than a mile, but it turned out to be the most terrifying journey either of them had ever made; her driving was atrocious. Shaking, she climbed out of the car, opened her handbag, took out her driving licence, and ceremoniously ripped it into little pieces. 'I'll never drive again,' she said. 'Why ever not?' asked the surprised archbishop. 'Because,' she replied, 'there is just so much traffic on the road!'

This story illustrates my point: if we do not see, it is because we are spiritually blind and need to do something about it. That is why we should examine our conscience each evening to pause for a few moments to review the day we have just completed. This examination is the time to ask God to show us everything we have done or failed to do that has kept him out. For it is this selfishness that prevents him from making his home within us as he ardently wishes and as Jesus promised the night before he died. After the examination, we should make an Act of Contrition for how we have failed in the past. A formal Act of Contrition could be used. Alternately, perhaps the recitation of what came to be called *The Jesus Prayer* can be said several times over, slowly and prayerfully: 'Jesus, Son of God, have mercy on me, a sinner'. Either way, make a sincere expression of personal sorrow. Then, make a firm purpose of amendment—a genuine decision to try to behave better in future.

CHAPTER 55

The School of Divine Love

I DON'T KNOW PRECISELY WHAT T.S. ELLIOT MEANT when he wrote that 'the end of all our exploring is to arrive where we started and know that place for the first time', but I do know what these words mean for me. The end of all my exploring, the end of all my speaking, and the end of all my writing ends up where I started many years ago. It is where the Church first started on the first Pentecost Day, almost two thousand years ago. It is the place where I have continually restarted after I have lost my way. I have come to know that place quite well.

In case you do not know the place to which I am referring as well as I do, let me set the scene for you. Although Jesus had risen from the dead, and the Apostles had seen him rise up and pass through a cloud on his way back to heaven, they were still afraid. They were still afraid that what their own political leaders did to him would be done to them, so they gathered together in the 'Upper Room', waiting for Jesus to send them the Love who would cast out all fear. This love would fill them with the wisdom that would enable them to begin building his Kingdom of Love on earth.

When they received this love through the person of the Holy Spirit, they could not contain themselves. They rushed out into the street to tell all and sundry what they had experienced. Three thousand or more Jews, who had come from all over the Roman Empire to celebrate the anniversary of the day when Moses gave God's Chosen People the Old Law to his people, were enthralled. They were not only enthralled by what they saw, but by what was said, and whom they were about to receive. For they understood what they were about to receive, a New Law, not written on tablets of stone, but onto and into hearts of flesh and blood. This New Law was God's Love poured into all hearts open to receiving it, enabling them to accept Christ and be taken up into him. They would be taken up into his Mystical Body and onward ever more deeply into his mystical loving. By that, I mean they would be taken into his mystical loving of his Father to receive his loving in return; they would also receive the gifts and fruits of his love.

When the three thousand saw what the Holy Spirit did for the Apostles, they asked St Peter how they could receive what the Apostles had received. The answer they were given was that, first and foremost, they should repent to have their sins forgiven and then they should be baptised. They were fellow Jews, so they knew what repentance meant. It was the recurrent clarion call of the prophets when calling God's people to prepare for the coming of the Messiah and the promised outpouring of the Holy Spirit that would follow his arrival.

For the Jews and, therefore, for Christ and the first Christians, there was no word for someone who had repented. There was only a word for someone who is repenting because it is a continual, ongoing process of turning back to God. The love received in return is given to the measure of the love they have been offering to God. This love will eventually enable them to become one with Christ—one in heart, one in mind, and one in body. More precisely we could say one with his Mystical Body and with his mystical loving of his Father. The first converts were told to be baptised in order to bring about this union, which nobody in the Old Testament thought even possible. Then, in, with, and through Christ, their continual repentance would be spiritually enriched beyond all their hopes and dreams.

Once drawn up into the Mystical Body of Christ, their continual repentance would draw them ever more deeply into Christ's prayer and into his contemplation of His Father. It was because they had been made in the image and likeness of God that both the Jews and the first Christians yearned for God with a love that, as St Augustine insisted, would be restless until it would rest in God. Prayer is the place where repentance is practised as we continually turn to God to be open to receiving all that God gives us. The different forms of prayer that change as we grow and develop in our spiritual journey are to help us to keep repenting—to keep raising our hearts and minds to God, enabling us to be always open to receive his love in return.

What I have called the *Asceticism of the Heart*, refers to the asceticism by which a person freely chooses to give quality space and time each day to practise repentance. In continually turning to God, this habit of repentance, in turn, leads to the continual mutual loving that finally leads to union with God. Means and methods of prayer—from the initial reciting of prayers and practising devotions to the prayer generated in the meditation that leads to contemplation—are like the props that keep a person's heart and mind open to God without ceasing. When Moses was watching his army from the mountainside, he opened his arms to pray for God's help. Noticing that the enemy began to thrive the moment his arms dropped, bystanders propped up his arms so that he would remain open to God, whose power would guarantee the victory that finally came. The props represent the means of prayer that, at different times in a person's spiritual journey, help keep the heart and mind open to receive God's grace.

Whenever we try to pray, we will always be tormented by distractions and temptations that will threaten to prevent us from raising our hearts and minds to God. However, rather than preventing us from praying, they actually help facilitate prayer. Why? Because the very essence of prayer is the repentance that is learned each time we turn away from a distraction or a temptation in order to turn back to God. Each time we turn away from a distraction to open our hearts to God in prayer, we have practised repentance. Thus, St Angela of Foligno called prayer the School of Divine Love since it is where the habit of selflessness is gradually learnt by practising a series of selfless acts. This habit eventually generates an inner disposition of heart and mind that puts the self second and others first. This disposition occurs particularly in prayer, where selflessness is learnt in trying to love God. Here, we open ourselves to receiving the love that will eventually transform us into the image and likeness of God.

CHAPTER 56

Spiritual Purification

USING THE SCRIPTURES FOR MEDITATION helps to develop a full-blooded emotional love of Christ, which suffuses our own weak human love. It surcharges it with a quality of loving that heightens our desire for union with God beyond anything we have previously received, and it keeps us in a state of religious enthusiasm *that has been called first fervour.*

It was this spiritual exuberance that enabled the first early Christian converts to help the Church through a transitional period from Judaism to which most of them originally belonged to the Christianity where they found their new spiritual home. As we well know, they did not jettison all they had learnt as Jews, and so many of their religious practices and prayers, as well as the psalms, canticles, and hymns they had used, were Christianised, while new ones were also generated. However, all were now centred around a new sacramental liturgy with the Eucharist at its centre, in which the whole of the Old Testament found its supreme consummation. Thus, the first Charismatic Christians, prominent in all the first Catholic communities, made such a vital and lasting contribution to building the spiritual and physical superstructure upon which the early Church thrived.

In the Eucharist, they took part in the profound religious liturgical rite in which their Risen Lord became present amongst them under the appearance of bread and wine. However, it was not just an appearance because the Christ with whom they yearned to become one was totally present in the bread and wine. Christ became present to them and also in them after communion. As the Council of Trent put it, Christ was present: 'body, blood, soul and divinity'. This weekly holy communion deepened their desire to be fully united with their Risen Lord, whom most of them had never seen in the flesh. So far, their meditation had enabled them to visualise him and love him as he once was, but the love that was generated within them wanted to be united with him fully—body, blood, soul and divinity. For this close and intimate union to be brought about, a deep and penetrating preparation would have to be endured in which not just their hearts and minds would have to be purified but also their bodies and souls to the very depth of their human being.

It is at this point, that the Holy Spirit leads a person out of meditation and into contemplation, where this purification takes place. A new method or means of prayer would have to be learnt to enable them to respond to the Holy Spirit, who would prepare them for union with the One who sent him in what St John of the Cross called *The Dark Night of the Soul*. I have already referred to this new form of prayer (or rather, prayers), but I want to refer to them again here because they are so simple. They are so simple that anyone can learn how to use them and, if my experience is anything to go by, many lay people have been using them for centuries without them ever realising it. St Augustine called these prayers *ejaculations*; others called them *prayers of the heart* or *spiritual arrows*.

These simple, short prayers represent their response to the God who is doing but one thing—the only thing that he always does, and that is loving. However, his loving at the beginning of the Mystic Way only highlights the sinfulness in them that separates them from the union that they desire. Unfortunately, without the spiritual direction that would teach them otherwise, they assume that God is not there, never mind loving them. As anyone who has loved anyone for long knows, this sense of separation is when real love is put to the test and practised in such a way that, if continued relentlessly, leads to perfect loving. Perfect loving means that you are continuously open to receiving love from the One to whom you have consecrated yourself. In human loving, despite the quality of your commitment, your love may never be returned, but in Divine Loving, it is always guaranteed.

At the beginning of what St John of the Cross calls *The Dark Night of the Soul,* the darkness believers experience and the distractions and the temptations with which they must contend seem to make nonsense of the promise that God is, nevertheless, always loving them. That is why St John of the Cross insisted that ninety percent of those who have come this far in their spiritual journey give up. If I were asked what has been the purpose of my whole life, what has been my apostolate in this world, then I would have to answer that it has been to convince genuine spiritual searchers that this is the key moment in their search for God's love. Then, I would encourage and inspire them to continue, when all human wisdom would suggest they are wasting their time and that they should turn their attention to doing something more practical.

This desire to focus our efforts on something deemed more meaningful is the strongest of the temptations; unfortunately, it usually succeeds in preventing the vast majority from journeying onward to receive the only love that can change their lives and ultimately transform and transfigure them into the image and likeness of the One to whom they have committed themselves. I have already and many times over tried to describe the historical reasons why the Mystical Theology that explains what is happening is no longer taught and why the spiritual directors who can help are not just thin on the ground but are almost absent.

Therefore, let me encourage fellow travellers with the truth. The first is that, despite all I have said, very many laypeople have been led to the beginning of mystical purification. Even without being told, they have adopted the short prayers appropriate for a person in the Mystic Way, but, as St John of the Cross predicted, they have floundered without clear and authoritative help. The second truth is that as the Holy Spirit has brought you to this point and wants to lead you on, he will do his part if you only do your part. Your part is to give exactly the same time to daily prayer as you gave before or would give if you were convinced that the Holy Spirit is leading you onward. As I have explained by describing my own journey, you will be asked to journey on in what the mystics have called *naked faith* because there is no feeling for a long time to confirm that you are on the right path.

This is how the desire for God that has been your spur from the beginning is purified and will enable you to pierce through the darkness of what a famous mystical writer called *The Cloud of Unknowing*. This symbolic cloud describes what seems to separate us from God and the union, in and through Christ, that we never had thought possible before.

CHAPTER 57

St Paul The Mystic

LET ME EXPLAIN THE TEACHING of The Cloud of Unknowing. It is so full of wisdom that the orthodoxy of this practitioner is above question. Those who have tried to reveal him as a counterfeit mystic have succeeded only in revealing themselves as non-practitioners. As the author of this famous work on Mystical Theology explains, the short prayer you make and keep making enables you to do two things at the same time. It acts like a prop enabling you to keep your heart's desire fixed on God, whom your faith tells you is on the other side of the Cloud.

Meanwhile, it also enables you to suffocate all the distractions and temptations that would draw your attention or what he calls *your naked intent* elsewhere. He then tells you to put them under what he calls *a cloud of forgetfulness*. For the foreseeable future, this practice is, your work in the daily time that you religiously give to prayer, like the early Christians before you who kept to their daily time for prayer come hell or high water.

Two words must begin to be seared into your mind and heart: *perseverance* and *immediacy*. If followed, these will guarantee you have done your part and will, therefore, guarantee that the Holy Spirit will do his part. Firstly, you must persevere no matter what you encounter in The Dark Night. No matter how dark it becomes, no matter how many distractions and temptations you must contend with, and no matter how long you have to face all that is within you separating you from God, you must persevere. Secondly, the very moment you find that your heart's desire is being drawn elsewhere, you must immediately turn back and open your heart to the divine love that this continuous action will enable you to receive.

The French Jewish Philosopher Simone Weil said that 'we are no more than the quality of our endeavour'. It is the quality of our endeavour in prayer that will determine the measure with which God's love can prepare and purify us for union with himself. In his monumental work, *A History of the Catholic Church*, Monsignor Philip Hughes uses one word to describe the early Christians' prevailing attitude of heart and mind: *renunciation*. They chose to follow Christ above and beyond all else; to do this, they renounced everything that could possibly prevent them from doing this day in and day out.

However, renunciation must be learnt and it is learnt by practising it repeatedly. The early Christians practised this repeatedly in the time allotted for personal prayer. This is the practical way in which they took up their daily cross and practised selfless, sacrificial giving. This sacrificial giving was most especially evident when they seemed to receive nothing in return. It was then that they united themselves with the selfless, sacrificial giving that was the hallmark characterising Christ's life on earth. As his daily dying to self led to Christ's Resurrection and Glorification, they knew that imitation of his daily self-sacrifice would lead to their own *white martyrdom*, but in God's time, not theirs.

Gradually and with perseverance, they enabled the Holy Spirit, to purify their hearts and their heart's desire too. Then, through using their hearts as a prism, they allowed the purification of the rest of their human being. The union for which they were being prepared

245

was for their minds, their bodies, and the whole of their human being. This fact is known and experienced by the great mystics, beginning even in this life, when their purification enables them to be led into the Mystical Marriage. Here, they tangibly experience God's love as it filters down into their bodies, making them ready and able to be united with the physical body of Christ. In the process, Christ's transformed and transfigured body transforms and transfigures their bodies too in the process.

The Mystical Marriage, the summit of spiritual life in this world, is preceded by what St Teresa of Avila calls *The Mystical Betrothals*. As the expression suggests, it is the Mystical Marriage, but only for brief periods until the requisite purification for ecstatic union has been completed. Like St John the Baptist, the first Christians realised that if they were to introduce Christ to others, they would first have to undergo a prolonged purification in a real or metaphorical desert. Therefore, while St Paul was preparing for ten years to become a true and effective apostle, his confreres in Jerusalem were doing the same. They did not write the details of their spiritual purification as later mystics did; nevertheless, this passage from St Paul's letter to the Corinthians is most revealing:

I know a man in Christ who fourteen years ago was caught up to the third heaven—whether in the body or out of the body I do not know, God knows. And I know that this man was caught up into paradise—whether in the body or out of the body I do not know, God knows—and he heard things that cannot be told, which man may not utter.

—2 Corinthians 12:2-4

A brief look at the chronology of St Paul's life enables us to see that, fourteen years before this letter to the Corinthians, St Paul was just completing his ten years of preparation and purification for his apostolate. St Paul could not have had such profound mystical experiences without such a purification, nor could he have received the wisdom that we find in his letters without the fruits of contemplation that shine through everything he wrote and did. Although we do not find similar details of mystical experiences in the writings of the other apostles, we do know that they experienced them, as we see the fruits of contemplation in all they wrote and did, as we can read in the Acts of the Apostles and the Acts of the Martyrs.

The same is true of the Fathers of the Church whose writings are still the bedrock of our Catholic faith. It is evident that today's Church is full of would-be apostles, eager to do what the first apostles did for the Church. Sadly, they are not so evidently prepared to do what their predecessors did. Both born Catholics and recent converts seem to think that a religious experience, albeit genuine, is a call to set out without delay to become the spiritual leaders for which they have not been prepared. The first apostles had profound and personal experiences of God's love. However, they still believed they had to spend many years of penance and repentance learnt in 'the desert' before they had the effrontery to set themselves up to lead and guide others.

Lest what I say is taken too literally, remember that St Catherine of Siena found her spiritual desert in her own home, where the success of her incredibly fruitful apostolate was made possible by years of continual prayer.

CHAPTER 58

Self-Sacrifice and the Mass

LET ME INSIST THAT WHAT WAS CALLED *'THE WAY* was not just for the early Church, but for all. At least, it is for all who can love and be loved and who want to make this their vocation by following Christ. That means for everyone, no matter who they are, how little education they have received, or what weakness of mind, heart, body or even what moral faults and failings they have been guilty of. The Way is for all because all have been made in the image and likeness of the living and loving God. St Peter was no intellectual but, rather, an ordinary working man who turned to fishing to support his family. Nor was he particularly outstanding for his holiness, at least not initially.

Do not forget that Peter denied Christ three times shortly before his Crucifixion. Yet he would become the Rock upon which the Church was founded. St Paul spent his time persecuting, torturing, and killing the first Christians before his conversion. Yet St Paul was the first to write the great secret of the spiritual life: your weakness, even your moral weaknesses, can become your strength. This astounding transformation from ordinary, weak men to extraordinary holy men willing to live and die for Christ is what The Way did for St Paul and St Peter and the other apostles, too, because God chooses the weak to confound the strong.

Therefore, I thank God for the dyslexia I once considered the curse of my life, for I now understand it has been my greatest blessing. All we need is the humility to see and accept our weakness and to keep turning back to God. In the words of St Peter, we must keep *repenting*. Once St Peter repented for denying Christ, he spent the rest of his life repenting and imploring others to repent as he did on the first Pentecost day. St Peter saw the time between Christ's first second coming as a time for repentance.

Throughout this time, our relationship with God involves continual and ongoing repentance, interrupted only when God chooses to make his presence felt by profound experiences of contemplation that take a person out of themselves. When this happens, we encounter God in experiences much like those St Paul encountered when he said that he had been taken up into the third heaven and into the Paradise Christ promised to the Good Thief from the Cross. St Teresa of Avila also refers to similar experiences by using words or expressions like *Full Union*, *Rapture* and *Ecstasy*. When these God-given moments of all-engrossing absorption into God occur, there are no distractions or temptations and, therefore for the first time, and, therefore, no necessity to continue practising the repentance to which they will soon have to return.

The very essence of all prayer we choose for every stage of our spiritual development is then the continual process of repenting. It is precisely by turning to prayer, a person can keep relentlessly turning back to God. It is in the act of continually repenting that our hearts are strengthened and our love is purified. This process of strengthening and purifying enables the love for which we supremely yearn to descend into us and to begin and continue to remake and remould us into the image and likeness of God as he is embodied in the human body of Jesus Christ.

Prayer becomes, for a Christian, as I have explained, what weight-lifting becomes for an athlete. Every time we raise our hearts to God, the spiritual muscles of our hearts develop, enabling us to pray with ever greater intensity and efficiency so that our hearts can expand to receive God's love in ever greater measure. Not only that, but something else gradually begins to happen. Our hearts become spiritual prisms that reflect and refract God's love into every part of our minds and our bodies so that one day we will be able to say with St Paul: 'I live, no it is no longer I who live, but it is Christ who lives in me' (Galatians 2:20).

In some forms of prayer, such as meditation, this weight-lifting can become easy and even enjoyable; however, contemplation can become increasingly difficult. When we find ourselves in darkness and beleaguered with distractions and temptations, it can feel like someone is putting ever heavier weights onto the bar we keep trying to raise; the continual temptation to give up becomes, at times, nearly irresistible. Yet, at times like these, we should be aware that we are travelling more swiftly than ever before. Opening ourselves more fully than ever, we are receiving more fully than ever before, the only love that is gradually changing us so that the impossible can become possible. Through the simple but ongoing acts of repentance practised in prayer, we can be made one with our Risen Lord and, through him, with the Father, who is our final destiny.

The lessons learnt in The School of Divine Love are also practised outside of prayer. Here, the acts of self-sacrifice first learnt become habits enabling us to continue loving God in others with whom we live and work outside of prayer. In this way, and without realising it, we unknowingly become the living, breathing embodiment of the man we meditated upon at the beginning of our spiritual journey and whom we will meditate upon once more at the end of our purification.

When the first Christians came together for their weekly Mass, the spiritual self-offerings that they had made individually and personally, both inside and outside of prayer, were simultaneously offered to God as a community to receive his loving in return. This regular communal offering bonded them together into an ever more vibrant and loving community that drew new converts in their thousands who could not resist the powerful magnetic force of God's love, alive and loving in other human beings.

What happened then in the early Church can and will happen again today if only those within the Church who have lost their way will listen to that single word uttered by St Peter on the first Pentecost day. Then, put what that word teaches us into practice every day of our lives, beginning now. For it is God's infinite loving, which is the fruit of repentance that can alone unite us with Christ and the family he founded on earth for the greater glory of God in this world and in the next. Who would believe it because it is so simple? Nevertheless, the truth of the matter is that the love learnt through continual repentance is the key to everything. This love is our personal fulfilment, holiness, and happiness, and that of the Church and the whole world for which Christ founded his Church.

I praise You, Father, Lord of heaven and earth that You have hidden these spiritual truths from the wise and intelligent and revealed them to little children.

—Matthew 11:25

CHAPTER 59

Paradise Regained

AT THE BEGINNING OF THE SWINGING SIXTIES, when I was completing my theological studies, the world of rock 'n' roll was stunned when a simple tune called 'In an English Country Garden' shot up to the top of the charts even before it was officially released. Even the Beatles were astonished that they had to play second fiddle to such a simple but captivating tune. But it was not just the tune, it was the words too that captivated the nation. Heaven consists of returning to a simple but beautiful garden. The ancient Jews were captivated by a similar yearning. They wanted to return to the beautiful garden that God first created for them. This garden was called Paradise, and here, the first man and woman lived in perfect harmony and bliss, not just with each other and creation but with God.

For in this garden paradise, Adam walked with God 'in the cool of the evening'. The Hebrew word used to describe this expression was *ruach*, the word used for the Holy Spirit. The term means 'the breath of God's mouth'. This Spirit of God communicated to all who, like Adam, were open to receiving God's very own life and love. God himself was the centre of this world, and human joy and happiness consisted of both walking and talking with God. It also consisted of revelling in an ongoing and loving relationship with him at every moment of every day. Each day centred in and around

God; and every time and every space was sacralised by the ongoing and ever-loving Holy Spirit, God's ever-present love that made their heaven on earth.

When Adam chose to seek self rather than God, Paradise on earth was lost and could be regained only by returning to the tender, loving relationship with God through a new Adam, Jesus Christ, the God-Man. When the early Christians came to be baptised, the first baptistries to be built were festooned with paintings, frescos, and murals depicting Paradise. They depicted the Paradise that the first Christians would regain, beginning here and now, in this life through the baptism that would take them up and into the 'New Adam' which was Christ, Risen and Glorified. When they went to their weekly Mass, their Mass was called 'The Heavenly Liturgy' because it was here that they received the 'New Adam' sacramentally, in whom they now lived and moved and through whom they could once more enter into a sublime union with God their Father through sacrificial loving.

At the height of Benedictine monasticism, the Cluniac Reform made their churches appear like the new Paradise into which Christians were called at baptism. In order to complete the impression, the Divine Office was sung nonstop for twenty-four hours every day of every week by dividing their communities into three rotating groups. Whilst one-third of the community praised God, another third worked, and the other third slept. They slept to refresh themselves to serve God in their daily work and then praised him through his Divine Office. The Divine Office was sung in their churches, which they beautified in such a way that they became the closest things in this world to the Paradise anticipated in the next world. When pilgrims flocked to their monasteries, it was to experience briefly here on earth what they would one day experience forever in heaven.

When Jesus was dying on the Cross, he promised the Good Thief would enter Paradise before nightfall, which was the very heaven to which he was returning himself. Thus, St Paul, in his sublime mystical encounter with Christ, said he found himself in what he called the third heaven, describing the place as Paradise. We can immediately begin the journey back into Paradise Lost. Yes, even here and now in this life, if we so choose, we can journey back by simply choosing divine love once more over the self-centred love that has been dominating our lives for too many years.

If St Paul was the first of the early Christians to tell us how he experienced returning to Paradise Lost, then St Peter was the first to tell us how to return there. Furthermore, because of her Immaculate Conception, Our Lady was the first to go back there through sublime Mystical Contemplation. What St Peter told us to do on the first Pentecost day is simplicity itself, although I do not say it is easy. He simply tells us to turn back to God, our true home, by repenting. In its most primitive form, this is what the word *repentance* means. *Repentance* is derived from the Hebrew word *shub*, which means *to return home*. Isaiah used it to mean *to turn back to one's Father* or *to return to the intimate union with God that Adam and Eve experienced in the first Paradise in the Garden of Eden*.

When Our Lady appeared to St Bernadette at Lourdes, she repeated the same message St Peter delivered at Pentecost. At Fatima, she delivered the same message, calling on us to repent, but she added a few more words so there could be no misunderstanding: 'You must repent and make sacrifices'. The first and most important sacrifice we must make is the sacrifice of our time. The sacrifices we make to set aside time for prayer must be remade many times over inside of prayer itself. We must be prepared to give up the time that we now give in Paradise Lost to give it to God. For it is here in prayer, that we must turn away from a myriad of temptations and distractions to keep repenting as we keep trying to turn back to God to open ourselves to receive his love. In prayer, we practise repenting more intensively than ever before as we keep trying to turn our minds and hearts away from self-love and self-indulgence to loving God.

God first promised to love us when he appeared to Abraham. Since then, he said his love was totally unconditional. God would never cease to love us, even though we may continually throw his love back in His face as we have done in the Paradise Lost in which we live. We can be united with God only by learning the same sort of selfless, unalloyed, unconditional loving that constitutes his very nature, for as St John has said, 'God is Love' (1 John 4:8). This love is the inner nature of his Son, Jesus Christ, into whose life and loving we entered at baptism, where we can be fully made one with him only by learning how to love as he did when he was on earth. Prayer is where we go to practise this sort of selfless, unconditional loving.

When you start giving time to prayer again after a long absence, or even for the first time, you will find that you must keep praying when you seem to get nothing in return, day in and day out. When you find, as you will, that this is your daily experience, you will be tempted to give up and turn away from prayer. Please be aware that if your immediate experience is not the presence but the absence of God, then this is the opportunity to begin to generate the selfless, sacrificial loving that was the very *raison d'être* of Our Lord's life on earth.

CHAPTER 60

A Catholic Renaissance

MORE RECENTLY, OUR LADY HAS APPEARED to tell us to take all our daily sacrifices to Mass on Sunday. Here, we offer them together with Christ's own simple, sacrificial, and unconditional loving which he offers to his Father. To the measure we give to God, he will give his love to us through Jesus in return. This love will contain all the infused virtues and all the fruits and gifts of the Holy Spirit. They will enable us to continue to repent, pray, and make sacrifices throughout the following week. Gradually, we are enabling Christ to sanctify and redeem us; then, through us, to simultaneously sanctify and redeem the world in which we live, as well as those who have chosen to return to him as a new remnant.

In order to help us to do this, we must learn from the prayer that Our Lady used and taught her Son to use daily. This prayer, which the ancient Jews and the first Christians called the *Shema*, is what we call the *Morning Offering*. In this prayer—like Mary and her beloved Son before her and all the first Christians—we consecrate the day before us. We do this in order to sacralise all we say and do so that we can unite ourselves in all we say and do with Jesus Christ. This sacralisation is how we practise the first and greatest of the new commandments—namely, to love God with our whole mind and heart and with our whole body, soul, and strength. As we try to do this, we are inevitably trying to put into practice the second of the new commandments, which is to love our neighbour as Christ himself loves us as we try to do everything for the honour and glory of God. *Ad maiorem Dei gloriam.*

Without us realising it we are also practising what Jesus called *The New Worship in Spirit and in Truth.* Unlike our Jewish forebears, we are not offering our precious livestock or home produce to God; we are offering ourselves and all we say and do each day. Nor are we offering these gifts in a Temple made by human hands, but in a New Temple made by the hands of God in, with, and through Jesus Christ, who is the new High Priest. He offers all we choose to offer with his own offering of himself in the New Temple, raised up on the first Easter day. Here, then, are the practical dimensions of the profound sacrificial and Mystical Spirituality, long since forgotten by us but practised by our first Christian ancestors as it was practised before them by Jesus Christ, who died a terrible and agonising death to introduce it to us through our first Christian forebears.

What we have to do next has already been said many times over. May God give us the grace to do it in these terrible times when, 2000 years after Christ first died for us, his beloved Church is in the process of spiritually disintegrating from the inside, possessed as it is by evil men of evil intent. Their pernicious practices cry out to heaven for the upcoming vengeance, which, according to Our Lady, is in the very near future! It may be too late to turn the *Titanic* around from her inevitable icy nemesis; however, it is not too late to save ourselves and those whom we love if we immediately return to the contemplative prayer, that is being asked of us, for it is never too late to love.

The Good Thief asked for mercy In the last minute of extra time, and Christ unhesitatingly forgave him, promising him the Paradise that we lost at the beginning, and he promised the thief he would enter it by nightfall. Be sure Christ will not deny us if we ask with a simple and pure heart, and then show, not just by our words, but by what we do, that we want to repent, make sacrifices and pray, as our first ancestors did before us. When we do this, then we will know his mercy and become the first new Christians to return as the New Remnant to the God-given spirituality he introduced to the early Church. Ultimately, we are called to save not only ourselves but also, as the New Remnant, to save the world. We save the world by heralding and birthing Christ the King again in this world through love.

When God first created our world, he created it in his Word or his Love, for his Word is his Love. He created this world of matter and form in space and time. Then into this world God's Love was made flesh because Mary, his immaculate mother, freely chose to become his mother. Our Lady has spoken in these unprecedented times when all that was once so promising is being destroyed. Tragically, those who have been in authority have not just been deaf to her words but positively stifled them. She has been calling on us to become like her by becoming mothers to Christ. We can do this only by freely choosing, as she did, to give birth to Christ again. To be Christ-bearers, we must begin now by trying to generate his love within us through selfless and ongoing unconditional loving, learnt in prayer.

In this way, we do what Mary, our Mother, is asking us to do—to become mothers to Christ so he can be born and rise again through us. Thus, he can rise again from the ashes of the Church, which so many modern Judas Iscariots have burnt to the ground. The future is in our hands because, in his goodness, God has chosen to redeem the world through us, for it cannot be redeemed without us. May God give us the grace, and may Mary, our Mother, bestow that grace on all who genuinely try to receive it. Then, through us, Christ the King will come again to the world that he chose to rule over through us.

But it must be said, as firmly as possible, that we can only move forward and become mothers to Christ, as Mary did before us, by preparing to take the radical steps necessary to change our lives through prayer. The Hermit, Sr Wendy Beckett, put it this way:

For spiritual reading there is only one test. It is not whether or not it sounds impressive. Style matters but this is only a means and can be used to self-glorifying ends. Nor is the test whether our hearts are touched. This too matters but emotions are volatile. It is so easy to read spirituality and in the reading deceive ourselves into thinking we live it. The only real test is whether what is written makes us love God more. Put it this way, the test is practical. Not whether we feel we love God more but whether we lay down the book and begin to consider what we must do. It is all in the doing that resolute activity that turns our vague longings into practice.

We may not be asked to give our lives for Christ, as were the early Christians in *red martyrdom*, but we are all called to daily die for him by accepting what they called *white martyrdom*. White martyrdom is practised through the daily dying to self we perform when we freely choose to give to God as a sacrifice the most precious commodity that we possess: our time given daily for prayer. In prayer, we must continually turn from the distractions and temptations in which our self-indulgence wants to wallow. This is the time we daily give to practising the repentance daily, which can alone teach us how to turn and open ourselves to God through endless self-sacrifice. Then, we receive from him the only love that can transform us into the image and likeness of his Son, Jesus Christ, Our Lord. As we progress, we will realise that we have been gradually transforming what was once secular space and time into sacred space and time.

We have long since forgotten the first proclamation of our faith when St Paul cried out, 'I preach Christ and Christ crucified' (1

Corinthians 1:23). In loving God through everything we say and do, we finally arrive at what the first Christians called, 'the prayer without ceasing'. In this way and in this life, we will progressively begin to play our part in transforming space and time, matter and form into the sacred so that we can return to the new Paradise from the Paradise lost where we now abide. Please know that we will be asked to take along with us all of those who see in us, as the first pagans once saw in our first forefathers, a true and new Christian world order. The Paradise that was once lost shall be made new and that making will begin in this current world until it is fully revealed once and for all as God's Kingdom finally arrives at last and Christ the King rules supreme.

Maranatha! Come, Lord Jesus!

Epilogue

WHEN I WAS CENSURED, like all whistleblowers, for drawing attention to the sexual abuse and cover-ups that were taking place in the Church in the 1980s, I withdrew into solitude. I believed that just as alcoholics have to hit rock bottom before they can admit their addiction and then begin their recovery and rehabilitation, the same would have to happen in the Church. When this happened, I hoped that the books that I wrote in my exile, detailing traditional Catholic prayer and spirituality, would be ready and available to those who wanted to restart their spiritual journey. Sadly, this never occurred. So, I simply continued praying and writing.

I became so lost in what I was doing that I became oblivious to what was in fact happening in the Church. I just assumed that self-disgust would lead sexual abusers and their allies, the concealers, to rock bottom, thence to recovery. What was indeed happening was something I could not imagine, even in my worst nightmares. Far from rejecting sexual depravity, a fiendish inner elite was not only bent on forgiving abusers and their allies without the sacramental absolution that they did not want anyway, but furthermore, they were intent on moving backward into neo-paganism! They were hell-bent on institutionalising and then even sacralising what had so recently been condemned as mortally sinful and taught to be so from the very beginning of Christianity.

261

In order to deceive, they continue to use traditional Catholic rites and rituals, Catholic language and terminology, so that the naive and the unwary would not notice that they are introducing 'the woke and wanton wisdom of the world' into a new Catholic pseudo-orthodoxy that that will support and collaborate with secular world leaders to usher in a new heinous world order called *Globalism*. Only God can help us, for only he can destroy the powers of Evil hell-bent on destroying the world he made to mirror his goodness, his truth, and his love. Prayer—true, deep, and life-changing prayer—is the only human action that can invite and maintain his presence within us. Then, he can vanquish once and for all the pernicious panoply and pandemonium that always reigns when evil-doing and downright devilry rules, where goodness, truth, and love once reigned before.

My first intimation of what was developing was in the autumn of 2015. Before that date, I was a fan of the new Pope Francis, who seemed full of promise, although I had not studied him any more deeply than reading his first, unalloyed hagiographers. I had been writing a column on prayer for the 'St Anthony Messenger' for the past fifteen years or so. A decade and a half was long enough for the editor to know my colours. It was long enough for him to know that I would not be the best person to write and enthuse about the 'Year of Mercy' that would be inaugurated that December on the Eve of Our Lady's Immaculate Conception. This proclaimed year was one of the first examples for the Universal Church to be treated to the double-speak that is meant to confuse. This papal action was meant to give the impression to traditional Catholics that it heralded and called for a return to Sacramental forgiveness as the first step toward future renewal and reform.

However, this proclaimed year meant something else entirely for the then-small group of elite, who were dedicated to radically taking over the Church in the name of the worldly wisdom of the modern world. It meant that God was forgiving them for all the sins they had committed as abusers, paedophiles, and concealers who had covered up their crimes. Furthermore, this merciful forgiveness was granted without them needing to ask forgiveness or ever receive sacramental absolution. Then, rather than this forgiveness being seen as a fresh start to turn back to God and the teaching that he had introduced into this world, it was something that can be described only as demonic.

This 'Year of Mercy' was to initiate a subtle revolution that would offer 'mercy'—nay, a free pass—to sexual abusers. Furthermore, this effort to reap the fruits of mercy, such as peace and hope, without undergoing the required contrition and penance was aimed at institutionalising and sacralising their gross sexual depravity. They used the Marx/Lenin principle originated by the Bolsheviks to take power during the 1917 Russian Revolution. Namely, a small group of people who know exactly what they want can take over the reins of power when all around them are in a state of confusion and bewilderment, if not total indifference.

The vast majority of Catholics, even the Catholic intelligentsia, have not realised what has been happening. It has been done gradually, furtively, but efficiently over the last ten or more years, long before I woke up to see what was happening. Now it is too late to stop the handpicked oligarchy from taking power in the Church, not just to introduce the woke and wanton wisdom of the world, but to join forces with those powerful and malign Machiavellian maneuverers bent on promoting a New World Order. This New World Order, otherwise called *Globalism*, will make the mediaeval feudalism we have long since escaped look like heaven on earth. For a fuller and more theological critique of the Synod, please read the letter sent by Cardinal Zen to his brother cardinals and bishops shortly before the Synod was opened, and then read the message of Archbishop

Carlo Maria Viganò for the 'Reawaken America Tour', published on October 14, 2023.

In order to move the Church toward a New World Order, the elite did not dare to call an Ecumenical Council when all the successors of St Peter would be called to Rome because they knew very well that the guardians of our sacred tradition would defeat them. Instead, they scheduled what they called a *Synod*—a gathering of handpicked and like-minded 'reformers' (or, more accurately, *revolutionaries*) who believed in their own form of 'totalitarian democracy'. In their form of democracy, what St Peter first called 'the people of God' were supposedly consulted. In fact, less than three percent of the Catholic population was approached, and the handpicked collators ensured that their token contributions were either ignored or reframed to coincide with the new conventual wisdom that now rules in Rome and will continue to rule. This new conventional irrationality will continue to rule like other totalitarian systems by what they call *Synodality*. In other words, it will be sustained by the self-same oligarchy who originally designed the revolution for their similar-minded successors so that the Holy Spirit, who speaks through them could be permanently marginalised.

When Native American Indians said that 'white man speak with forked tongue', they did not know that their words were prophetic. Such words were prophetic not just for themselves and for their people but for all future people who are consistently being lied to one day after the next, not just by individuals but by global institutions bent on doing to humanity what was once done to native American Indians. As one brave once said, 'When you came, you had the Bible, and we had the land; now we have the Bible, and you have the land'.

The double-speak used by the revolutionaries has served them well. Opposite ideals are presented, sometimes in the same sentence, to induce a sense of safety and security for the traditionalists while simultaneously satisfying the dreams of the revolutionaries. The bees must be sedated for the hornets to take over the nest. American Indians did not write books, but George Orwell did, and if you want to know what is happening to the Church, read *Animal Farm* and *1984* and apply those themes to what is happening to our Church today.

Beware of the elite's insidious ways of using traditional language to dupe the naive and the unwary into believing that nothing is changing. In fact, the tectonic plates on which our faith depends are being ruthlessly removed by heretical autocrats to be replaced by sand—the sinking sand that the Gospels warn leads to disaster. Beware, for although the victory that Christ promised will indeed ultimately prevail, the gates of Hell will nevertheless have their fling.

Become a member of the New Radical Remnant by doing only one thing—the one thing necessary. That one thing is to open your mind and heart to God like never before. Then, keep turning to him day and night. Keep opening your heart and mind to him in ever-deepening prayer. When we do this, he will take over your lives, our lives, and through us, destroy this, the worst and most pernicious plague ever to have ravaged our beloved Church. It is indeed the worst ever precisely because it has come from within, like a thief in the night.

Be sure that many will be flung into the hell of hopelessness, and despondency may seem to reign supreme. Take heart, however. If you want hope, then let me assure you that the Man who rose from the dead on the first Easter day is alive, in control and loving us right now. Although he is even more wounded today than he was then, he is still radiating with his all-unconditional and all-conquering love for those who are prepared to radically turn to receive it. But beware, Infinite Love is not true love if it is not ultimately

265

complemented by justice. And if Our Lady of Fatima and her other more recent prophecies are to be believed (and who would doubt her?), justice will begin in this world and likely in the very near future.

BV - #0037 - 071124 - C0 - 229/152/16 - PB - 9781965801031 - Gloss Lamination